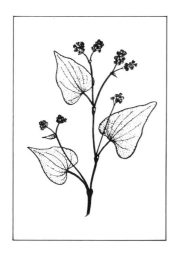

MAN'S
USEFUL
PLANTS

INCLUDING

FOODS AND

BEVERAGES,

MEDICINES,

ARROW POISONS,

PERFUMES,

FABRICS,

WOOD,

PAPER,

RUBBER,

WAX AND DYES

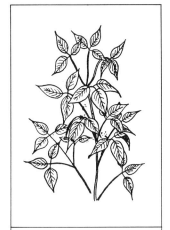

MAN'S USEFUL PLANTS

MICHAEL A. WEINER

MACMILLAN PUBLISHING CO., INC.
New York
COLLIER MACMILLAN PUBLISHERS
London

Macmillan Publishing Co., Inc., 866 Third Avenue, New York, N.Y. 10022
Collier Macmillan Canada, Ltd.
Printed in the United States of America
1   2   3   4   5   6   7   8   9   10

Library of Congress Cataloging in Publication Data

Weiner, Michael A. Man's Useful plants.

Bibliography: p.

1. Botany, Economic—Juvenile literature.
[1. Botany, Economic. 2. Plants] I. Title.
SB107.W44   581.6'1   74–18469   ISBN 0–02–792600–1

FOR MY SON
RUSSELL GOLDENCLOUD
WHO BOTH FOLLOWS
AND LEADS THE WAY

ACKNOWLEDGMENTS

The field of economic botany is an ancient one. Fortunately, several scholars have preserved the accumulated information and have added to this body of knowledge through their own investigations. To these men I am grateful. The standard works by Edlin, Hill, Hvass, Sargent and Schery have been freely referred to and are acknowledged in the bibliography.

I am indebted to Professor R. E. Schultes for opening this field to me through his writings. Without access to the library of the Botanical Museum of Harvard University, this book could not have been written.

CONTENTS

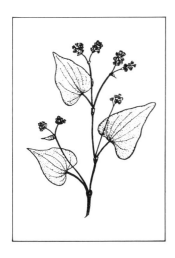

MAN'S USEFUL PLANTS

INTRODUCTION

To those of us who buy our food in stores, heat our homes with fuel transported over long distances or pick our clothing from long and neatly ordered racks, sitting and enjoying the beauty of nature may seem to be the most perfect use plants can afford.

Early man, however, did not have much time to sit and gaze at trees and flowers. He was busy gathering food from trees, first the easily picked fruits and leaves and later the bark, roots and seeds to see if they, too, could sustain him.

When he discovered fire, he began to use grasses, shrubs, vines and trees as fuel. Fuel to light the torches that became the first effective weapons against mammoths, tigers and bears. Fire to keep him warm, to make food delicious, to harden the points of spears and arrows. Fire to lead him through a world of darkness.

Some of our primitive ancestors emerged from cave dwellings and began to build shelter from the tough, flexible trunks and branches of their wooden allies. In warmer climates men lived under the protective canopy of the forest or in the trees for safety from prowling beasts.

Man the hunter needed tools or weapons. Not content with just throwing stones, he invented an early version of the tomahawk by tying stones to a tough stick with vines. Eventually our hairy and resourceful ancestors poked and prodded, sniffed and tasted almost every fruit and leaf that attracted them. Some, no doubt, died or became violently ill from poisonous plants, but the most intelligent groups learned to distinguish the safe and even tasty plant foods from the dangerous or deadly.

People get sick, even some of the toughest people of the most primitive tribes. To cure sickness, to treat the pains of wounds, early man turned to the confusing tangle of the plant world as well as to the animals for medicine. It was then believed that "like cures like" and that for every illness there existed a cure. Primitive healers often selected plants on the basis of shape or color. Leaves shaped like the human liver were used to heal disorders of the liver; a piece of gnarled wood was used to treat convulsions, and so on. By learning to recognize the signs of the plant world, early doctors believed they could cure most illnesses. Although today medicine is no longer practiced according to such a simple theory, many of our most important medicines still come from plants—plants that grow beneath the sea, along the shores, upon the rocks of running streams and in the woods, fields and deserts.

Clothing was originally made from the skins of animals,

The leaves of this plant, which are the same shape as the human liver, were thought to be effective in treating liver disorders.

but later it was woven from the fibers of stems, seeds and leaves. Today fibers spun from the same natural sources are increasing in demand.

Some men found less practical applications for certain plant products. Not only were berries eaten, but their juices were used as paint. Our ancestors often decorated themselves with bracelets and beads from polished nuts and seeds, and music was played on instruments crafted of wood and other vegetable products. Even today primitive music is played on instruments of gourds, wood, stems and reeds, and the finest string instruments in modern orchestras are still made of wood.

Slowly the use of plants evolved from foods and fuel to weapons, shelter, clothing, medicine and thousands of other products. As time progressed, inquisitive man attempted to use every resource, whether of animal, mineral or vegetable origin. In doing so, he learned to perfect his techniques and to extract the most useful products with the least effort.

Today great industries spin on products of the soil, and some of these products are described in this book. Before looking at them, we should orient our thinking along the lines of the present "energy crisis." Is our supply of food and other essential products that are derived from plants subject to a "plant crisis"? Will we be faced with a shortage of grains and vegetables, as well as a loss of some of man's favorite spices, such as pepper, mustard or cinnamon? Will gradually have to give up beverages that are made from plants, such as tea, coffee, chocolate, beer, wine and some soft drinks such as cola and ginger ale?

If the supply of plants on which we depend for food becomes short, we may wonder about those other products and delights that are very much a part of our civilization and are often essential to our survival. Will the plants from which we make many important medicines—such as penicillin, digitalis, birth-control pills and the opium-derived pain relievers—begin to disappear in the immediate future?

Are we beginning to see shortages in other plant-derived products as well, such as fabrics and clothing made of cotton and flax, ropes and thread made from Manila hemp and paper, plastics and other products that are derived from wood or cellulose? Is rubber in short supply? Are there any other sources of rubber besides the few species that are presently cultivated in South America and the Far East? Since soaps, paints, varnishes, lubricants, candles and cooking oils are made from many useful oil plants, are we to lose these products in the event of a future "plant crisis"?

In an attempt to answer these questions, this book describes many products of the plant world and the plants from which they are derived. While the reader learns to appreciate some of the many ways in which he is dependent on the plant kingdom, he may come to realize that the plant world is a resource that must be nurtured carefully, lest a wide-scale loss of useful plants occur.

Plants are not finite, in the sense that they either renew themselves or are propagated by man or other animals. However, should man lose the foresight of the most intelligent of his species and fail to protect the world of plants—abusing it instead through overuse or neglect, chemical fogs or fires, or simply by paving over too many natural areas—he will lose not only many products and foods but those places to rest and dream which make life worth living.

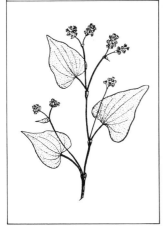

FOODS

AND

BEVERAGES

Although many of our foods come directly from plants, most of us also eat animals or animal products. Butter, eggs, milk, cheese and yogurt come from animals, as do meat, fish and poultry. But the animals that provide these foods also have eaten, and their food is directly or indirectly of plant origin. We may enjoy a ham steak, but the pig has developed from a vegetarian diet. The natives of Siberia may depend solely on reindeer meat, but these beautiful animals subsist on tiny plants called reindeer moss that grow beneath the snow.

Some of the animals eaten by man are themselves flesh-eating creatures. Certain fish eat smaller fish; lions eat gazelles and other smaller animals. But the smaller fish eat plankton, a marine plant, while gazelles eat leaves and grass. If we trace the food chain of any animal, we will see that ultimately it depends upon a plant. Plants provide us with all our food, indirectly as the base of all food chains or directly in the forms described in this book.

The value of foods is often expressed in terms of the vitamins, minerals, fats and oils, carbohydrates and proteins they contain. Vitamins are important in preventing diseases such as beriberi, pellagra, rickets and scurvy. Their role in maintaining a general state of good health and in preventing other diseases is only beginning to come to light. The work of two internationally acclaimed scientists, Albert Szent Gyorgyi and Linus Pauling, indicates that from ten to thirty times the amount of vitamin C presently recommended in the daily diet may be able to prevent the occurrence of the common cold and other infections. [Publisher's note: Their views are very controversial and you should consult your physician before taking more than the recommended daily requirement of vitamin C.] Fresh fruits and vegetables and whole-grains are the best natural sources of most vitamins, although vitamins B_{12} and A are generally available only from animal foods. The green parts of most beans and peas contain some vitamin C, while cabbage, broccoli, parsley, chili peppers and sweet peppers are very rich sources of this vitamin.

Minerals are required by the body in small amounts and can be secured mainly from animal foods, which are particularly rich in iodine, potassium, iron, calcium and phosphorus. Leafy green vegetables are also especially rich in the required minerals.

Fats and oils are fuel foods essential for the release of energy. They also help in the absorption of vitamins A, D, E and K, and they help insulate the body against cold. Oils are available from both plants and animals. Plant fats are particularly abundant in coconut and oil palms, olives, sesame seeds, peanuts and soybeans. Butter, lard and fish oils are some common animal fats.

Carbohydrates (*carb-*/carbon; *-o-*/oxygen; *-hydr-*/hydrogen) are found in starchy foods such as the cereal grains, in staple root crops such as the potato and in all sugars. They provide the energy necessary for activity. Few people are deficient in carbohydrates because they are widely available from many foods, including most nuts.

Proteins are necessary for the proper growth and repair of the body's tissues and muscles. In fact, proteins are the base of the entire structure of all body cells. These nutrients are available from animals and plants, but animal proteins contain more of the essential amino acids (the chemicals out of which proteins are made) than plant proteins. Vegetarians must rely upon the occasional intake of meat, milk, fish, poultry or food supplements to obtain all the essential amino acids.

CEREALS AND OTHER GRAINS

No Blade of Grass, a recent film, depicts the horrors of a famine in England brought about by the death of just one family of plants, the grasses. As the story begins, all pasture grasses are destroyed by a virus. This results in the starvation and the death of all livestock. The people reassure themselves by saying they will just have to do without meat, milk and eggs for a while. They ration their remaining supplies of these commodities, but they begin to understand that the chief cereals and other grains on which they have depended since the beginning of their lives have also been invaded by the deadly virus. All the important grains belong to the grass family. Panic ensues as millions of people fight for survival, searching for a few wild plants and the food crops that have escaped the deadly virus.

Corn, wheat and rice are grasses, as are barley, oats, rye, sorghum and millet. Without the nutritious seeds of these plants, the majority of the world's people could not survive. Fortunately, *No Blade of Grass* was not based on an actual event. It is unlikely that any one virus could successfully invade all members of a particular family of plants. Nevertheless, the film touches on a major truth, the dependence of civilized societies on the grasses.

In the Temperate Zone millions of people rely on wheat for baked goods and macaroni products; in Asia millions exist mainly on rice; while in South America and eastern and southern Africa corn is still important in the diet of large human populations. Throughout the world no family of food plants is as heavily utilized as the grasses.

The grains, especially rice and wheat, provide more humans with essential nutrients while satisfying hunger than any other foodstuff. Because of this they are termed *primary staple foods*. Corn and other grains are also staple foods for many millions, as are the bulky root crops, but not for the great numbers of people who rely upon wheat and rice. Corn and the root crops are therefore termed *secondary staple foods*.

Staple foods are grouped separately from *accessory foods*, of both plant and animal origin. We must remember that many accessory foods—such as meat, fish, poultry and many types of nuts, peas and beans—may be just as nutritious as the above named staples (if not more nutritious), but they are not available to enough people at the present time to be considered primary staple foods.

WHEAT

The gentle sway of a field of wheat being rustled by the wind remains a picture of prosperity for wealthy nations of a temperate climate.

Until recent times the entire wheat grain was used as food after being ground between two stones, but since the latter part of the nineteenth century wheat has been ground by a series of steel rollers that remove all the nutritious brown coat, known as bran. What remains of wheat after it has been processed and stripped of its most valuable components is "refined" white floor. The most nutritious portion of the original wheat grain, the bran, is often used for feeding cattle, while man has generally chosen the poorer portions of wheat for himself.

How is it that scientific man with his knowledge and intelligence is able to produce far more wheat per acre than the early farmer but is not able to feed himself the most valuable portions of this crop, choosing instead to feed them to animals?

Brown breads, also known as whole-grain breads, contain

all the nutriments of the original wheat germ and husk. Compared to whole-grain breads, white bread is little more than a nutritionless lump of starch. It is difficult to understand why brown breads were abandoned for white breads, but one theory is that the milling companies, which first introduced white flour to the consumer, decided to "push" white breads soon after they realized that wheat grains with their nutritious embryos removed were less troublesome to grind on high-speed rollers. Bread makers also discovered that flour stripped of its live embryos would stay fresh much longer.

The English writer Geoffrey Bowles best states the argument for a return to unprocessed brown or black flour. The same reasoning applies to unrefined brown rice, which is so much more nutritious than white rice. In the British publication *Countryman* [as it appears in *Cooking with Wholegrains* by Mildred Orton, New York: Farrar, Strauss & Giroux, 1971] Bowles says,

> The best food chemists are the earth and the sun, which produce the wholewheat that the steel rollers of the white flour millers spoil. . . . food is stuff to be eaten fresh, not to be "kept" as if it were an heirloom. . . . wholemeal flour naturally does not "keep" because the grain in it is alive. Germless white flour "keeps" because it is dead . . . all its original goodness having been sifted out of it.

Fortunately, many people are presently insisting on baked goods that have been made with whole-grain, stone-ground flour; the flour of our early American ancestors. This is the best use for one of the world's most valuable plants.

Many hybrid wheats have been developed that produce far greater yields than did the earliest cultivated varieties. More than 400 million acres of prime farmland are used for growing fourteen or so wheat varieties every year. This important food crop is grown in most countries in the Temperate Zone, from the equator to the Arctic Circle. In terms of world production, the Soviet Union produces the most wheat, with the United States, Canada, several European countries, India, Turkey, Argentina, Australia and China producing most of the remainder. Of course, crop failures do occur and these natural disasters change the order of world productions. A recent crop failure forced the Soviet Union to buy huge quantities of wheat from the United States at great political expense to both governments. This is an especially keen example of the way in which plants so often affect the lives of individuals and governments.

RICE

For most people in tropical and warm temperate regions rice is by far the most important of the food grains. More people rely upon rice as a food staple than any other plant in the world. Unfortunately, most of the grain's value is removed during milling, when it is converted from brown to white rice.

On a typical American rice farm, such as those in Texas, Arkansas, Louisiana and California, the harvested rice is first dried with heated air. This process, which removes from 13 to 14 per cent of the moisture in each grain, makes the rice easy to store. After drying, the grains are stored or transported to rice mills where they are processed. Brown rice consists of the "unpolished" grain, which means that only the outer hull is removed. The bran, which contains the outer cuticle layer and the germ of the rice, is not removed. This rice bran contains niacin and other vitamins.

The bran and other layers of the grain, such as the inner cuticle layer and portions of the rice kernel itself, are removed to make white rice. This product is nutritionally poor and is usually "enriched" with iron, thiamine and niacin. Unfortunately, white rice that has been "enriched" still lacks some of the vitamins that are contained in plain brown rice.

Beriberi, a disease caused by insufficient intake of the B vitamins, is still common in countries where "polished" white rice is the dietary staple. Although the B vitamins are present in rice before processing, the large processers remove the brown husks and part of the kernel and use it as cattle feed. Only the starchy white grains are left for human consumption.

TABLE 1
Nutritional Comparison of Brown and White Rice
(Sample quantity: 100 grams each of brown and white rice, cooked)

	BROWN RICE	WHITE RICE
Water (percentage)	70.3	72.6
Calories	119.0	109.0
Protein (g.)	2.5	2.0
Fat (g.)	0.6	0.1
Carbohydrate (total) (g.)	25.5	24.2
Fiber (g.)	0.3	0.1
Ash (g.)	1.1	1.1
Calcium (mg.)	12.0	10.0
Phosphorus (mg.)	73.0	28.0
Iron (mg.)	0.5	0.2
Sodium (mg.)	—	—
Potassium (mg.)	70.0	28.0
Thiamine (vitamin B$_1$) (mg.)	0.09	0.02
Riboflavin (vitamin B$_2$) (mg.)	0.02	0.01
Niacin (a B vitamin) (mg.)	1.40	0.4
Tocopherol (vitamin E) (mg.)	8.3	—

Source: Rice Council of Houston, Texas.

Unlike any of the other major food grains, most rice varieties must have a swampy habitat for much of their life cycles. It takes about six months from the time of planting until rice is ready for harvest. In Asia, where much rice is grown by ancient methods, the level of water in the rice paddy is kept just below the upper leaves of the plant until flowers begin to appear. At this stage the water level in the fields is lowered to encourage the plant to produce large seeds, even though the leaves, stem and root begin to wither as they dry. Adverse conditions may cause organisms to produce large or even more potent seeds to ensure survival. When the rice grains have grown to their maximum size, the plants are cut by hand. The seeds are threshed by being shaken in a grated tray, while the valuable seed coats are allowed to fall away.

In the United States—where only 1 per cent of the world's total crop is produced—highly mechanized procedures enable the farmer to grow more rice per acre than can Asian farmers. However, mechanized production requires huge amounts of gasoline for tractors and equipment, as well as expensive manufactured fertilizer. Traditional Asian methods may be less productive in the short run, but in the future, when man has exhausted most of the gas and oil for operating his machinery, he may have to return to the traditional methods of growing and harvesting rice that are still practiced in Asia and other "underdeveloped" regions.

Man may develop new methods for producing his food supply, but in the final analysis he is always dependent upon the good graces of mother nature. The recent failure of a crop of so-called "miracle grain" rice in countries that adopted modern methods to grow this new variety was the result of a great drought. Mechanization is desirable if we are willing to pay the costs in terms of energy, resources and pollution. However, we must never lose the capacity to fall back upon primitive methods of raising our food if we hope to be able to avoid widespread famine.

Traditional rice fields in Indonesia.

Rice shoots being planted in an
Indonesian rice paddy.

Mechanized harvesters cut and collect wheat
on a farm in North Dakota.

This woman is making *tortillas*—flat, dry pancakes made of corn meal.

CORN

Cultivated maize or corn is the native American's greatest contribution to the world's supply of food. Maize, which is believed to have originated in the lowlands of central South America many thousands of years ago, is a descendant of a wild variety of pod corn. First domesticated by South American Indians, thousands of varieties came into existence during the time of the great Inca civilization. By the time Columbus discovered America, the cultivation of corn had spread through Central America and Mexico north as far as Canada. It was grown wherever Indians practiced agriculture, and for many tribes it was a basic part of the daily diet.

Corn is a fairly nutritious food, some varieties being more than 12 per cent protein. Today most corn is used for cattle feed, with the United States producing nearly half of the world's crop.

Where corn is still an important food for humans, as in parts of Africa, Latin America and southeastern Europe, it is prepared in several interesting ways. Africans generally grind corn with a mortar and pestle, later boiling the corn meal with water to form porridge or gruel. The Italians prepare a similar food called *polenta*. *Tortillas*, a favorite food in South America and Mexico, are flattened cakes of ground corn meal.

Although North Americans today commonly eat only corn as a cooked vegetable, as popcorn or as a cereal, the Iroquois Indians had at least twenty-three different corn recipes, some taking several days to prepare. These included leaf cakes, hominy, paper bread, batter husks and corn beverages.

Barley, rye and oats are considered minor food grains of the grass family because the number of people who depend upon them as dietary staples is less than the great majority who rely upon the "big three" grains—wheat, rice and corn. Nevertheless, in some parts of the world these minor grains are still primary food sources.

Barley was the most essential cereal to the ancient peoples of Asia, Africa and Europe. It has since been largely replaced by wheat and rice. Barley is one of the hardiest of the grasses and is still grown in the Andes Mountains of South America at altitudes as high as eleven thousand feet and in the Soviet Union as far north as the Arctic Circle. In parts of northern Europe and isolated regions of Asia it is considered a staple crop.

The principal use of barley today is as a highly nutritious livestock feed. The grains contain as much as 13 per cent protein. A substantial portion of the world's crop (over 30 per cent) is germinated and turned into malt, which is used in the brewing of beer and other alcoholic beverages, as well as in various breakfast foods, sweets, candies and syrups.

Rye will grow in soil too poor, at altitudes too high, and in temperatures too cold to support most other food grains. Although it is a relative of wheat and barley, it is grown at altitudes well beyond the limits of these other grains. In parts of northern Europe and Russia rye is grown on lands above fourteen thousand feet in elevation.

Rye bread (also known as black bread in Europe) is the main food product of the grain. In Scandinavia a crisp type of rye bread is highly valued for its low caloric content and its indefinite keeping qualities. Over 95 per cent of the total world crop is grown and used in Europe, where the rye plant is primarily used for hay and pasturage for animals. It is sometimes fermented to produce alcohol for industrial purposes as well as for making rye whiskey, gin and beer.

Oatmeal, porridge and grits are highly nutritious because the oat grains from which they are made may contain nearly 14 per cent protein and 4 per cent fat. Israeli plant breeders have created an experimental oat grain that contains nearly 30 per cent protein.

Oats are primarily grown to feed horses and other domesticated animals. The principal growing regions are found in the United States, Russia, northern Europe and Canada.

SORGHUMS

Sorghums resemble corn but are more highly resistant to drought and grow in all warm countries. The grains are a food staple in tropical Africa, China and parts of India, where they are ground up and consumed as mush or in the form of pancakes. In the United States sorghums are grown chiefly to produce livestock and poultry feeds.

MILLETS

Millets are grown throughout Asia and Africa, where they are eaten daily by millions of people. They are highly resistant to drought and are primarily grown in semiarid areas under primitive conditions without the aid of modern fertilizers or machinery.

After their stalks are cut, usually by hand, millet seeds are threshed and then either boiled or ground into flour. Nutritionally millets are about equal in food value to rice.

WILD RICE

Wild rice is primarily uncultivated, growing naturally along the banks of lakes and slow-running streams in the northeastern United States. These highly valued grains are gathered mainly by Chippewa Indians on their lands in northern Minnesota. Although wild rice is no longer an important food of the Indians, they are the principal gatherers, eating much of it themselves while selling some to the lovers of gourmet foods who are willing to pay high prices for grains that are actually no more nutritious than the more commonly obtainable varieties.

BUCKWHEAT

Buckwheat, a native of central Asia, produces small seeds that are ground and used as flour for soups and porridge by millions of people in Poland and Russia. Buckwheat is consumed in the same manner as the other cereal crops described in this section but is technically not grass. It is related to weeds capable of growing on poor soils and is popular in regions that cannot support other grain crops.

The quinoa plant is a dietary staple among Indians in the Andes Mountains, where it still grows wild. The white, red or black seeds mature in five or six months and are eaten whole after toasting or in soups or are ground into flour used for making *tortillas*, cakes and porridge. These highly nutritious grains, also not members of the grass family, are produced by an herb and consist of up to 19 per cent protein and 5 per cent fat.

The above-named cereals are the most important sources of plant food for man. They may be eaten directly as cereals or indirectly in the form of meat and dairy products after being consumed by livestock.

The last two grains, buckwheat and quinoa, are termed "pseudo-cereals" because their seeds are not surrounded by husks like the other cereal crops, which are all members of the important grass family.

LEGUMES, NUTS AND OILS

Next to the grasses, the bean family contains more useful food plants than any other plant family. Peas, most beans and lentils belong to this group, and they contribute significantly to the nourishment of millions of people throughout the world. Although most nuts and oil plants belong to various other plant families, they are grouped here because they are often the seeds of plants like the beans and peas and they are equally valuable sources of food.

Proteins are often lacking in the diet of people who cannot secure adequate amounts of animal or plant foods rich in these essential nutrients. Beans, peas and nuts are especially rich in protein, and attempts are being made to make them available on a wider scale and at a lower cost, both to the undernourished people of the world and to those in different nations who are unwilling or unable to pay the high price of meat or fish.

BEANS and PEAS

Beans and peas are also known as legumes. All plants in this large family are characterized by pods that open along two sides when the seeds mature. The bean family includes widely diverse species of vines, trees, shrubs and herbs that grow in different environments, ranging from wet forests to desserts. Legumes are grown easily, mature quickly, and have nutritious seeds that store easily owing to a low water content.

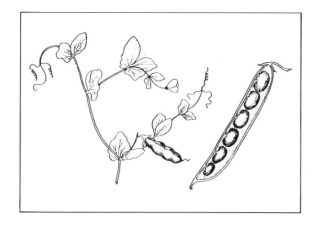

Garden pea vine with pod (left) and kidney bean pod (right).

The roots of many legumes contain bacteria able to use nitrogen in the air to form nitrates and then protein. Because of this special "nitrogen-fixing" ability, many legumes can be grown without the use of expensive nitrogen-containing fertilizers. Because all parts of these plants, including the seed jackets (pods), contain much protein, those parts not eaten by man are valuable as livestock feed. In addition, the leftover plant parts are often plowed back into the soil and left to decay. By releasing large amounts of nitrogen, they serve as valuable fertilizers.

Next to cereals, the seeds of legumes (beans and peas) provide more people with protein than any other group of plants, and legumes are between two and three times richer in protein than the cereals. The seeds also contain fats and carbohydrates, minerals and vitamin B. They are especially important in regions where little animal flesh is available.

Forage crops, such as alfalfa, clover, sweet clover, kudzu, lespedezas and the vetches, are also legumes. These plants are extensively cultivated as food for animals but are also used to improve farmland when they are plowed back into worn-out soils.

ALFALFA
CLOVER
SWEET CLOVER
KUDZU
LESPEDEZAS
VETCHES

Table 2 lists some important legumes, their uses, origin, and regions where they are principally grown today.

TABLE 2 *Principal Legumes of the World*

TYPE OF LEGUME	USES	NATIVE TO	PRINCIPAL REGIONS OF GROWTH	AVERAGE PROTEIN CONTENT
SURFACE LEGUMES:				
Pea	Animal feed, human food	Central Asia and/or Southern Europe	U.S.S.R., China, India, U.S.	23%
Chick-pea	Important food in principal regions of growth	Western Asia	India, Pakistan, North Africa, Spain, South America	17%
Kidney bean (common green bean)	Human food, animal feed	South America	Worldwide	25%
Lima bean	Human food	South America	All warm climates, including southern U.S.	7.6%
Cowpea (black-eyed pea)	Seeds eaten fresh, frozen or canned; dried seeds ground into flour; green pods sometimes eaten	Central Africa	Important crop in Africa, India, China, but also grown in all warm climates, including southern U.S.	23%
Soybean	Extremely important human food; oil has wide application	Southeast Asia	U.S. and China	40%
Broad bean	Livestock feed, human food	North Africa	Italy and other European countries, Mexico, Brazil	25%
Peanut	Human food, animal feed, hay, salad and cooking oil	South America	India, West Africa, China, Indonesia	30%
Lentil	Seeds cooked in soups; also excellent meat substitute	Southwest Asia	India, Pakistan, Southwest Asia, North Africa, Southern Europe	25%
TREE LEGUMES:				
Mesquite (*kiawe*)	Honey from flowers; cattle feed	West Indies; Mexico; Central America	Scattered throughout warm, arid regions worldwide	N.A.*
Carob	Candy, flours, gum, stock feed	Syria	Mediterranean countries	4.5%
Honey locust	Rich livestock feed	Eastern U.S.	Eastern U.S.	N.A.*

*N.A.–information not available

The soybean and peanut are important examples of surface legumes, plants that grow on or in the soil or climb on other plants or other erect objects. The carob is an example of a tree legume, one of those few species that bear nutritious seeds inside pods. Tree legumes are highly recommended as plantings in the vicinity of cultivated soils because of their ability to check erosion with their wide-spreading roots. Their seeds and pods are an excellent stock feed and fertilizer.

In terms of nutritive value no plant compares with the soybean, which is 30 to 50 per cent protein. Lean beef is 19 per cent protein, while lean fish from the sea averages 17 per cent protein. For more than four thousand years the Chinese, Japanese and other Asian people have relied heavily on soybeans for their protein. Many recipes have been devised for cooking these tough beans, some requiring elaborate procedures. They can be prepared simply by mashing and boiling for several hours or by roasting. In Japan the familiar soy sauce is prepared from boiled, split, fermented beans blended with salt and wheat. The Japanese dish *miso* consists of rice that has been inoculated with special bacteria or fungi and then fermented with cooked soybeans and salt.

SOYBEAN

Soybeans were first introduced to the United States in 1804, but they did not become important until the 1930's, when they became the second largest cash crop in the Midwest. Today the United States produces nearly two-thirds of the world's crop, or 20 million tons each year, while China accounts for one-third.

The entire soybean plant is used as food—for its oil, which constitutes the base for much margarine—and as a protein cake for animal fodder. In China the soybean is especially valued as food, fodder, lamp oil, lard substitute, coffee substitute and as a lubricant for machinery. It is even used in the manufacture of paints, varnish and lacquer.

PEANUT

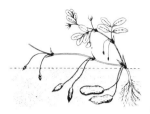

The peanut is a legume, not a true nut, because its shell is actually a pod. Unlike other beans or nuts that grow above ground level, peanut pods are found growing beneath the soil. Also known as the ground nut, this legume ripens its pods underground. This protects them from most animals and also acts as a self-planting mechanism that ensures the growth of new peanut plants during the following season.

Originally native to South America, where it was a plant of major importance (peanuts are represented on pieces of ancient Peruvian pottery), the peanut is today grown principally in West Africa, India and China, three countries with a protein-deficient diet. Over half of all the peanuts grown in the United States are made into peanut butter. Peanut oil, which is removed by pressing the nuts, is a popular cooking oil and also important in the manufacture of margarine. Peanut oil cakes, which are pressed from leftovers in the above manufactures, are valuable cattle feed.

CAROB

The seed pods of the carob, a small evergreen tree of the Mediterranean, are rich in protein and are often ground into a popular "health food" flour that is used in making cakes, bread and candies. It is especially valued by those who love sweets but are allergic to chocolate. Carob flour is also eaten dry in its native habitat.

In ancient times the hard carob seeds were known as carats and used as weights on scales in the evaluation of the value of gold and silver. Diamonds and gold are still measured in carats; 24 carats is pure gold.

NUTS

Nuts have been part of man's diet from the time he first began to forage for his food. Although they are presently underutilized as primary sources of oil and protein, they have great potential for feeding the world's undernourished peoples.

There are several reasons why nuts are eaten less frequently than grains. Many years must elapse between the time nuts are planted and harvested as marketable crops. They are somewhat bulkier to store than grains and require more labor to harvest and process. Nuts also contain a great amount of oil, which causes them to spoil quite rapidly unless preserved or dried.

In the United States nuts are eaten mainly as snacks and their food value remains unappreciated, while in some parts of the world they have been highly utilized for centuries. In Europe acorns have been eaten since ancient times, and in Spain and Italy they are still ground into flour that is used for baking bread. In southern Europe chestnuts have long served as food. The nuts are ground into flour and used in soups, stuffings, stews and porridge or eaten after roasting or boiling or are preserved in sugar. In South America brazil nuts are an important native food.

ACORNS
CHESTNUTS
BRAZIL NUTS

Nuts are excellent supplementary or accessory foods, and some of the interesting, unusual and important varieties are summarized in Table 3.

One of the most important plants in the world, not only for food and oil but for a myriad of other uses as well, is the coconut palm. Considered by some a sacred plant, it provides the world with many products. In the tropics this useful tree provides thatching for shelters, fibers for brushes, mats, ropes and brooms and fuel for lamps. An alcoholic drink called toddy is sometimes made from the sap that is tapped from the top of the trunk, while a so-called "millionaire's salad" is occasionally taken from the top shoot, even though this kills the tree.

COCONUT

During World War II it was discovered that the sterile liquid found inside fresh young coconuts could be used as an emergency substitute for blood plasma. Some native Fijian doctors have even shown that surgical operations heal

TABLE 3 Edible Nuts of Commerce

NUT	BOTANICAL SOURCE	NATIVE OF	PRINCIPAL REGIONS OF GROWTH	NUTRITIVE VALUE (OF FRESH NUTS)			REMARKS
				% of Protein	% of Oil	% of Carbohydrate	
Acorn	Many species of oak trees, wild and cultivated	Many countries in the Temperate Zone	Spain, Italy, Greece and other Mediterranean countries	—	—	—	Once a staple of many early American Indians. After removing tough exteriors and bitter-tasting tannins, acorn meal was baked into bread or used for porridge, soups, etc. Is still an important food among poor Europeans in the Mediterranean countries.
Almond	Small tree related to the peach, wild and cultivated	Eastern Mediterranean	Spain, Italy, Australia, South Africa, California	20	55	17	The large seeds of a peachlike fruit. While we eat the outer flesh of the peach and throw away its inner seed, with almonds we eat the seed and throw the flesh away. Used in cooking and eaten raw.
Brazil nut	Trees up to 150' in height, wild only	Amazon forests of South America	Brazil and Venezuela	17	67	07	Brazil nuts are really the seeds found inside the large woody fruits of giant trees. Amazon natives have long used these nutritious nuts as food.
Cashew	Small, gnarled trees, wild and cultivated	Dry lands of eastern Brazil	Wild trees grow throughout tropical America. Cultivated trees are grown in India, Africa, Mexico, Florida, and southern European countries	17	46	29	Cashews grow at the base of pear-shaped "fruits" or peduncles. The extracted oil is used in cooking. Cashews are eaten raw and used in preserves; and the juice of these nuts is fermented into wine.
Chestnut	Trees up to 100' in height, cultivated	Eastern U.S., Japan, China, southern Europe	Spain, Italy, France, Far East (U.S. trees destroyed by chestnut blight)	06	05	42	Chestnut trees will grow on hillsides too dry to support any other food plant. In southern Europe the nuts are ground into flour used in soups, stuffings, stews and porridge. In the Far East they are often boiled and eaten like potatoes.

Coconut	Palm trees, wild and cultivated	Malay Archipelago	06	51	28	One of the most useful plants of the world. Discussed in detail in this section. In the U.S. dried coconut is widely used in cakes, pies and candies.
Hazelnut (Filbert)	Shrubs in U.S., larger trees in Europe and Asia, cultivated	North America, Europe, Asia	16	65	13	Hazelnuts are mainly grown from the European trees, even in America. The native American shrubs are not commercially important.
Maca-damia	Tall evergreen trees, cultivated	Northeastern Australia	8	70	16	Macadamia nuts are shelled, dried, boiled in oil, salted and vacuum packed. They are very popular where grown and expensive owing to the lengthy period of growth (7 years to full maturity).
Pecan	Wild pecan trees grow up to 100' high; cultivated varieties are less than 50' high. Nuts originally obtained from wild trees, now principally from cultivated varieties	Southeastern U.S., Mexico	11	71	13	Pecans are popular in candy, ice cream, baked goods and as dessert nuts. They contain more fat than any other plant product.
Pistachio	Small tree with evergreen leaves, wild and cultivated	Syria	22	54	16	Green pistachios are salted and often dyed red. Used as a supplementary food and as a flavoring for ice cream and confectionery.
Walnuts	Tall trees and smaller trees, all very handsome, wild and cultivated	Eastern U.S. (black walnut), eastern U.S. and Canada (butter-nut), Iran (English walnut)	18	65	13	Black walnuts were a favorite food of eastern U.S. Indians. Principally gathered from wild trees and mostly used in ice cream and confectionery. English walnuts are the common table variety; their shells are easily removed, unlike the other varieties.

better when incisions are sewn with sterilized coconut fibers in place of catgut.

Coconuts hang in bunches at the tops of slanting palms, and workers must sometimes climb seventy-five feet to reach them. The tasty white flesh is eaten in the tropics, while a refreshing drink can be obtained from the liquid inside the tough outer shell. Throughout the tropics people harvest coconuts on plantations, both for local consumption and for shipment abroad. Before tourism became a source of income, many Pacific Islanders relied solely on copra (the dried white flesh) for their cash income.

After removal from the nut, copra is either dried in the sun or in an oven that is usually fired by burning the discarded husks as fuel. Dried copra is the source of coconut oil, which is used in the manufacture of margarine and as a cooking oil. It is made into shredded coconut for cooking. Dried copra also makes an excellent livestock feed after the oil has been removed.

OILS

Oils pressed from many nuts and seeds are among the most widely used plant products. Some of these are edible and find use as salad or cooking oils as well as in the production of margarine, shortenings and mayonnaise. Plant oils are also used to make paints, varnishes, linoleum, soap, shaving cream, cosmetics, ink, waterproofing material, candles, disinfectants, illuminants, putty, tar, artificial leather, rubber substitutes and lubricants.

Vegetable oils are categorized into four main classes: nondrying oils, semidrying oils, drying oils and fats. Nondrying oils generally remain liquid on exposure to air and are edible, but they are also used for making soaps, lubricants and other industrial products. This group includes castor oil, olive oil, peanut oil and the oil extracted from almonds, avocados, cashews, filberts and other minor sources.

Semidrying oils dry slowly on exposure to air, forming a soft film that makes them useful for making some paints, soap and candles. Some of these oils are used for illuminating lamps, while others are edible as well. This group of slow-drying oils includes corn oil, cottonseed oil, sunflower oil and sesame oil. Minor sources of semidrying oils are the seeds of apricots, brazil nuts, citrus fruits and species of pine, rice and tomatoes. Colza and rapeseed oils are occasionally used in the manufacture of soaps.

Drying oils dry rapidly on exposure to air, forming an elastic film that makes them particularly important in the manufacture of paints and varnishes. Some of the drying oils are edible and are widely used as cooking and salad oils and in the production of margarine and mayonnaise. The quick-drying oils include linseed oil (from the flax plant), safflower oil, soybean oil, tung oil and the oils from candlenuts, grape seeds, hemp seeds, poppyseeds and walnuts.

All of the above categories of vegetable oils are considered unsaturated fats. They remain liquid at room temperature. The fourth category, not yet discussed, is comprised of saturated fats and includes the principal vegetable fats: coconut oil, palm oil and cocoa butter. Saturated fats are all solid at ordinary temperatures.

Highly saturated fats (think of them as thick and solid) are believed to be a contributing factor in many heart and circulatory problems. Medical researchers generally advise that cooking be done with vegetable oils that contain unsaturated fatty acids (think of them as thin and fluid).

Although not all medical authorities agree with the theory that oils containing many unsaturated fatty acids are less likely to cause heart and circulatory trouble than those containing highly saturated fats, there is enough interest in this question to list some common fats and oils in the order of their relative saturation.

Highest in Polyunsaturated Fatty Acids	Highest in Saturated Fatty Acids
Walnuts	Coconut oil
Safflower oil	Chocolate
Corn oil	Lamb fat
Soybean oil	Butter
Salmon	Beef fat
Cottonseed oil	Shortenings
Peanut oil	Pork fat
Liquid corn oil	Lard
	Egg yolk
	Chicken fat

In general, liquid vegetable oils should be used in cooking by those who prefer diets low in saturated fatty acids. Both butter and margarine, which are solid at room temperature, are relatively high in saturated fats.

POTATOES AND OTHER STAPLE ROOT CROPS

Plants that store the food they require for new growth underground are known as root crops. Underneath the soil the food is safe from most animals, with the exception of the pig, man and other avid diggers. It is also safe from surface droughts, physical injury and the cold.

In this section only those root crops that are staple foods of large human populations are described: the white potato in Ireland, the cassava in many tropical countries, the sweet potato and taro in the Pacific Islands and yams in regions of West Africa.

Other root crops include the onion, leek, garlic, beet, radish, turnip, parsnip and carrot. Few people rely upon these vegetables as their food staple but eat them instead for their vitamins and quality of taste. They are all treated in the section on vegetables.

WHITE POTATO

Grown originally in the moist highlands of the Andes, the white potato was brought to Europe by the Spanish conquistadors before the sixteenth century. It took another one hundred years before the value of this plant was appreciated by the Europeans. By the 1700's the potato had become widely planted throughout most of Europe, and in Ireland it eventually became the only food for some people.

Legend relates that either Sir Francis Drake or Sir Walter Raleigh first brought the potato to England and presented the vegetable to Queen Elizabeth. After growing it in the royal gardens, the kitchen staff, unfamiliar with the strange food, gathered and cooked the green leaves and placed them before Her Majesty. Unknown to the staff, the stems and leaves of potatoes contain poisonous sap, but fortunately the leaves were so bitter that the queen rejected them. When called to account, the nobleman supposedly saved himself by explaining that only the large tubers were supposed to be eaten.

It is not surprising that all green parts of this plant contain some poison. The potato family contains many poisonous and medicinal species, including belladonna, jimson weed, black henbane and tobacco.

Botanically the potato is actually a stem, not a root, but for convenience the vegetable is always included with root crops. Potatoes are nearly 80 per cent water and 18 per cent starch, the remaining 2 per cent consisting of protein, many essential minerals, some fat and cellulose.

To see what this tuber is composed of, peel and chop a raw potato and then soak the pieces in cold water. Squeeze all water from the soaking pieces into another container, and two separate liquids should appear: a clear liquid on top, a white sediment beneath. The clear fluid contains albumen, also found in egg whites. It also contains fat, sugar, gum and minerals. If you pour off the clear fluid and heat it, the albumen will coagulate. The white sediment is starch. If it is left to dry after the clear fluid is poured off, it will crack like dried mud. This substance is presently used in the paper, textile, confection and adhesive industries, where starch is required.

Much of the world's potato crop is used for cattle feed, but in the Soviet Union, Poland, and northern Europe it is consumed daily by large numbers of humans. In the United States more potatoes are used for making potato chips than are cooked and eaten as a vegetable. Nevertheless, throughout the world the potato is only slightly less important as a food staple than rice and wheat.

New potatoes are presently grown from planted sections of the tuber that contain "eyes," or buds. They are a popular crop because they grow easily on most soils and produce a high yield per acre. Unfortunately, potatoes contain so much water and so little protein that they must be considered less valuable as a crop than wheat, rice and corn.

A potato blight caused by a fungus infection in Ireland in 1845 was responsible for the death of half a million people and the migration of another one and a half million people to the United States. Today spraying and dusting are responsible for controlling leaf blight and other plant diseases in this important food crop.

The English word *potato* is taken from the Indian word for the plant, *batata*. More nutritious than the white potato, the sweet potato contains about 2 per cent protein, 5 per cent sugar (which gives it a sweet taste) and substantial amounts of iron, calcium and vitamins.

SWEET POTATO

Sweet potatoes are quite popular in the southern United States, while in Japan they are now second only to rice as a food crop. In the New Guinea highlands these potatoes play an important role in the life of many villagers. Many ceremonies revolve entirely around the growth of this important root food. Throughout the South Seas, Indonesia, Japan and China it is a primary food staple.

Sweet potatoes are the swollen roots of a vine that trails along the ground. They are often confused with yams, which are the roots of climbing vines. Sweet potatoes are propagated by using pieces of the roots, whole roots, or sections of the vine placed in the soil, and they are harvested in four to six months. In Japan they are raised between rows of grain crops to keep the soil in better balance, each crop taking and putting back different minerals.

CASSAVA (TAPIOCA)

The cassava is an example of a plant that is poisonous to eat in its raw state. Its edible properties were probably discovered through long and costly trials by ancient man. To eliminate the dangerous prussic acid present in the raw tuber, cassava is thoroughly dried in the sun or sliced and boiled. It is often eaten like potatoes; whole, mashed or fried. In Brazil cassava is prepared in a dish called farina, which resembles corn meal. It is usually eaten by the poorest people who cannot afford even corn. Originally cultivated by South American Indians, this plant now constitutes a primary food for many humans in Central and South America, the West Indies and some regions of Africa and the Far East. Unfortunately, although cassava is very popular, it is not very nourishing. The South Pacific Commission is attempting to persuade people in the islands of the South Seas to forgo these starchy roots in favor of more nutritious root crops such as taro, yams and sweet potato.

The cassava plant became popular in the tropics because it grows easily on poor soils that will maintain few other food plants. This crop is typically cultivated in jungles that have been burned away to clear land for planting. The massive tubers, which sometimes weigh up to twenty pounds, contain little more than starch and water. They are less than 1 per cent protein.

YAMS

Yams are particularly important in West Africa and Southeast Asia and to a lesser extent in the Pacific Islands and the West Indies. They easily grow from buds, or "eyes," and can be stored for longer periods than most tropical foods. The yam plant is a climbing vine, and it needs a stake, tree or other support to grow around. About eight to twelve months are required from planting until harvesting. Yams are generally peeled and then boiled and mashed; sometimes they are roasted, fried or ground into flour.

Just as the white potato has been a staple in Europe and the sweet potato a staple in many tropical countries, the taro has been a food staple throughout the Pacific Islands.

In villages throughout Melanesia a dish of these large boiled roots is served steaming hot with every meal. Accessory foods served with taro include fish, some meat and many vegetables, including cooked green taro leaves. In Hawaii taro paste is a favorite traditional dish. *Poi*, as this paste is called in Hawaiian, is made from boiled taro roots that are pounded and then fermented for a few days. This food is still sold in modern supermarkets in Hawaii and is a very popular baby food because the fine granules of starch it contains make it easy to digest.

Sugar cane is unloaded at a processing mill in Costa Rica.

SUGAR PLANTS

All green plants manufacture some sugar. Most plants use this sugar in their own life functions and store little that can be harvested by man. Several plants store large quantities of sugar and therefore are man's most frequently used sugar plants. Among them are sugar cane, sugar beets, maple and other minor sources of sugar.

Sugars are stored in roots, stems, flowers and fruits. Root sugars are found in beets, carrots, parsnips, turnips and other underground vegetables. Beets are by far the world's principal root sugar crop. Stem sugars are derived from cornstalks, sorghum stems, sugar canes and the trunks of sugar maples. Sugar cane is the main source of stem sugars. Flowers contain nectar that bees convert into honey, and fruits owe their sweetness to the presence of sugars.

The three main types of sugar are sucrose, from sugar cane and sugar beets; glucose, principally from grapes; and fructose, from most fruits.

Most of the world's refined sugar is derived from sugar cane and sugar beets. Maple, palm and other sources of sugar are described because they do provide much sugar for local consumption in many parts of the world.

SUGAR CANE

Most sugar used in the United States is obtained from sugar cane, a tropical grass that grows from ten to twenty feet high. These bamboolike stalks grow from large rhizomes. After about fifteen months of growth, the plant produces a large, silky tuft of flowers. When the flowers begin to wilt,

the sugar content of the cane is highest, about 12 per cent of its total weight. Sugar cane is harvested at this stage of growth.

In industrialized plantations cutting is accomplished with large machines that are driven across the hot, dusty fields. Where the work is done largely by hand, as in Cuba, Asia and India, laborers swing long machetes to cut across the hard stalks. The rhizomes that remain in the ground normally produce two or three more crops in subsequent years.

The cut cane is transported from the fields to large mills, where it is crushed into many pieces and then passed through a series of steel rollers. These rollers press out the sweet sap, leaving a dry residue known as bagasse.

The sweet juice is first strained to remove some of the large impurities such as dirt and shreds of bagasse. It is then boiled to remove the proteins—of all things! Lime is added to prevent sucrose from changing into other, less desirable forms of sugar as well as to aid in the removal of other impurities. The juice that remains is ready for concentration and conversion into sugar. It is boiled again until it becomes a thick syrup; when left standing, it crystallizes into raw sugar, which is dark brown in color. The sticky material that remains is known as molasses.

Raw sugar is "refined" into white sugar in a series of treatments that remove valuable protein, minerals and organic acids along with the particles of dirt. The brown sugar commonly sold in supermarkets is merely refined white sugar that has been rewashed in molasses. Although it is slightly more nutritious than white sugar (owing to the addition of molasses), it is not as rich as raw sugar. Interestingly, in many rural cane-growing regions raw sugar is consumed by the workers, who thus receive some good nourishment.

Aside from molasses, which is useful as a food and in making candy, the other sugar by-product, bagasse, is useful in several ways. It can be burned as fuel, converted into fiberboard or paper or mixed with molasses to form an excellent livestock feed. Conservationists in many tropical countries are encouraging sugar growers to increase the utilization of this by-product in order to reduce the need to dispose of bagasse by burning, which causes great clouds of smoke, a serious form of air pollution.

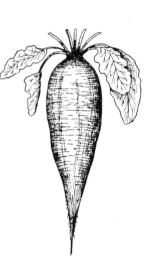

People living in temperate climates seldom realize that the sugar they use directly, granulated or in cubes, or indirectly, in canned fruit, juices or cookies, may come from the sugar beet, a plant that grows in climates too cold to sustain the tropical sugar cane. Sugar beets are botanically the same plant as table beets; however, sugar beets have large roots, shaped like carrots, while the roots of table beets are small and round.

To become independent of the sugar cane grown in the tropics by the British, Napoleon I of France ordered his scientists to develop a source of sugar from a plant that could be grown in a European climate. Beets had been used as a source of sugar since before the birth of Christ, but never on a large scale. With Napoleon's backing, interest in the sugar beet was revived.

At that time wild beet roots contained only 5 to 7 per cent sugar. Today, as a result of selectively growing only those beets with roots especially rich in sugar, sugar beets contain about 15 to 20 per cent sugar.

To extract sugar, the beet roots are washed and shredded and the pieces soaked in tanks of heated running water. This process, known as diffusion, removes 97 per cent of the sugar, in solution with water. The remaining sugar is pressed out of the pulp that remains. The sugar solution is treated with lime, carbon dioxide and sulphur dioxide to produce crystals of sugar chemically identical to cane sugar. Both are composed of sucrose.

Beet-sugar by-products include molasses, which is used as livestock feed and in the production of industrial alcohol; the filter cake, left over after the juice is purified, which is a useful manure; the pulp, which is an excellent stock feed; and the green top leaves, which are used for feeding cattle and as fertilizers.

Two-fifths of the world's sugar is derived from sugar beets. The major producers are Germany, France, Poland, the Soviet Union and the United States.

SUGAR MAPLE

While Europeans relied upon sugar cane and sugar beets to sweeten their foods and beverages, the native Americans used the sweet sap of the sugar maple.

To withdraw sap from maple trees, the American Indians simply made a gash in the trunk about two inches deep and one foot long. They then drove a flat stick into the bottom of this cut and collected the flowing sap in bark or clay containers. To make sugar, the Indians placed heated stones in the maple sap until it boiled and became a thick syrup. The syrup was then allowed to freeze overnight, and the next day the ice that formed was skimmed off the top. This process slowly removed water from the sap; gradually it thickened until only solid crystals of sugar remained.

Maple sugar and syrup were highly esteemed by the Indians. The Iroquois carried their syrup on journeys in empty quail and duck eggs. Other tribes made a food to consume during their long travels by mixing syrup or sugar with ground corn. This nutritious food was easily stored for long periods of time and needed no preservatives.

The early settlers adopted the Indian methods of producing maple sugar and syrup and eventually improved on them. They hung pails from trees for a sap collection. Because the pails were metal, they made it easier to boil down the syrup. Unlike the wood and bark vessels of the Indians, they could be subjected directly to the heat of fires.

Today, although some people still enjoy the expensive maple sugar that is harvested mainly in New England, the industry is slowly disappearing because of rising production costs and the destruction of maple forests.

Interestingly, maple sugar is chemically identical to cane and beet sugar; all are composed of sucrose. The different flavor of maple sugar comes from impurities that enter the sugar from the tree.

Other Sources of Sugar

Sugar is also obtained on a small scale from various palms that are grown commercially in India and to a lesser extent in Africa and several Asian countries. These include the wild date palm, the palmyra palm, the coconut, the gomuti palm and the toddy palm. Except for the date palm, which is tapped in the stem, these palms are tapped by cutting off the flower stalks at their tips. About three to four quarts of sap a day can be collected from each palm for up to six months. Palm sugar is obtained by boiling and cooling the sap.

WILD DATE PALM
PALMYRA PALM
GOMUTI PALM
TODDY PALM

A variety of the grain crop known as sorghum yields a syrup that is also used as a sweetener. Sweet sorghum, as this plant is called, is grown primarily for local consumption in many countries. The plant juices are pressed out of the stems and used mainly in the form of syrup for cooking.

SWEET SORGHUM

Honey is made by bees from plant nectars that contain the sugars sucrose, glucose and levulose. The nectars are partially digested by bees and converted into honey, a storage product, which contains the sugars fructose and glucose. The taste of honey varies according to the kind of flowers visited by the honeybees, each kind of flower imparting its own flavor. White clover honey is regarded as superior to that made from sweet clover, while buckwheat honey is darker and more strongly flavored. In the tropics honey from orange blossoms is highly regarded, as are the sweet-flavored honeys of papaya, logwood and kiawe.

Sweeteners have been coveted by man as early as biblical times. The description of a "land flowing with milk and honey" indicates a time of prosperity. Honey remained the only form of sweetening until a sweet syrup was extracted from bamboos during the late Roman period. Throughout the Middle Ages sugar remained a luxury item, available only to the very wealthy. Since the seventeenth century sugar has been in great demand throughout the world.

Although sugar was once considered a "perfect food," useful for "quick energy," many reputable medical researchers have been attempting to convince the public that sugar may be undesirable and possibly even dangerous. Evidence indicates that sugar reduces the body's supply of B vitamins and disrupts calcium metabolism. Dentists have long advised against consuming this "useful" product, and if present medical research can be projected into the future, sugar may decrease in popularity until once again honey becomes man's principal sweetener.

FRUITS AND VEGETABLES

FRUITS

Fleshy fruits were among the first foods eaten by early man. Readily available, tasty, filled with thirst-quenching liquid, fruits have remained a favorite food through the ages.

Wandering bands of men first gathered edible wild fruits to satisfy their hunger. As time passed, they selected the tastiest and largest varieties to put under cultivation. Orchards provided a more reliable source of food than was available by randomly searching through the forests. Today many of the same wild fruits are still eaten, along with the many cultivated varieties.

Fruits that are grown in temperate climates consist mainly of water; about 80 per cent is average. The remainder is sugar, some useful salts, cellulose, organic acids and vitamins. These fruits, which include apples, apricots, blueberries, cherries, cranberries, grapes (and raisins), peaches, pears, plums, strawberries, tomatoes and watermelons, are seldom food staples and are eaten for their flavor and vitamin content.

Fruits are also used to make refreshing drinks, and the following early American recipes may be of interest. They first appeared in *The Practical Housewife*, published in 1860, and appeared again in 1966 in *Early American Beverages*.

APPLE ADE:

> Cut two large apples in slices, and pour a quart of boiling water on them, strain well and sweeten. To be drunk when cold or iced.

APRICOT DRINK:

Take a pint of the juice of bruised apricots, filter until clear, and make into a syrup with half a pound of sugar, then add one ounce of tartaric acid, bottle, and cork well. For a tumbler 3 parts full of water, add two tablespoonfulls of the syrup, and a scruple of carbonate of soda, stir well, and drink while effervescing.

CHERRY DRINK:

Prepare the same as apricot, substituting the cherry juice for the other fruit.

ORANGEADE:

Squeeze out the juice of an orange, pour boiling water on a little of the peel, and cover it close. Boil water and sugar to a thin syrup, and skim it. When all are cold, mix the juice, the infusion, and the syrup, with as much more water as will make a rich drink. Strain through a jelly-bag, and ice.

In the tropics fruits are often staples and sometimes the only food. Some staple tropical fruits include the banana, breadfruit, coconut, date and fig. There are hundreds of edible fruits in the tropics, and some that have, or are beginning to have, a North American market are described. The durian and lychee are included because of their importance in the regions where they are grown.

ACEROLA
(BARBADOS CHERRY)

Acerolas have recently become favored by "natural food" lovers because among all fruits they are the richest natural source of vitamin C. Linus Pauling, a Nobel laureate, recently published his theory that vitamin C, when taken in large quantities (1000 to 4000 milligrams daily), acts to prevent the occurrence of the common cold. [Publisher's note: Many other distinguished scientists and physicians disagree with this theory.]

These small, acidic fruits grow on trees in the gardens of

many homes in the Caribbean countries. People eat them fresh, cooked, or sell them to large canneries where the delicious red juice is pressed and then sealed in cans. Acerola plantations have been operating in Puerto Rico for about thirty years and produce the bulk of the commercial crop. The fruit is also cultivated in Texas, Florida and Central America through northern South America and is harvested to some extent in these regions.

AVOCADO

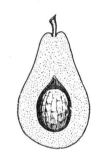

Due to their relatively high protein content (1.7 per cent), avocados are becoming increasingly important in the United States, where they are mainly eaten raw, in salads. In terms of energy and food value, avocados have more nutriments than an equal amount of meat. They are also rich in fat, carbohydrates, iron and vitamins.

This valuable but highly perishable fruit has been an important part of the everyday diet in Mexico for thousands of years. The small trees that bear the pear-shaped avocado are cultivated on a fairly large scale in California and Florida.

BANANA

Almost every native village in all warm climates has a small garden of banana trees for local consumption. A convenient and tasty fruit, the banana is a staple in many diets. Bananas contain carbohydrates, fats and 1.2 per cent protein. They are considered one of the world's best foods, having three times the food value of wheat, and because they are very easily digested, they can even be fed to babies.

With the development of refrigerated ships, this fruit became popular throughout the world. Bananas destined for distant markets are cut while green and allowed to ripen after arriving at their destinations. As the fruit ripens, it becomes yellow and its starchy mass turns to fruit sugar. While North Americans usually eat bananas raw, people in tropical countries often cook them and make a flour from the dried, unripened fruits.

Native to India or Malaya, the banana is one of the world's

earliest cultivated crops. It is presently grown in all warm countries (except desert regions, which are too dry), and Brazil is the leading banana producer for the U.S. market. Other exporters to the United States include Central and South American countries, Africa and India. Many varieties of banana are also grown and consumed in tropical Asia and the Pacific Islands.

BREADFRUIT

Although rarely seen in American markets, the breadfruit, is a staple in the diet of many Pacific Islanders. The novel and subsequent motion picture *Mutiny on the Bounty* is based on the true story of a mutiny that occurred during the attempt to transplant the breadfruit from the island of Tahiti in the Pacific to the island of Jamaica in the Caribbean in 1778. The British hoped to replace the banana as a dietary mainstay among their colonized peoples because they believed the breadfruit would be less expensive to cultivate. After the *Bounty* left Tahiti, mutineers set the ship's captain, William Bligh, adrift with a few loyal men. Bligh managed to survive incredible hardships and reached safety after traveling over one thousand miles in an open longboat. He commanded a second ship to Tahiti for a new supply of breadfruit seedlings and this time was successful in returning to Jamaica. However, breadfruit never did become popular in Jamaica, and the only lasting "transplants" of these voyages were the mutineers who hid successfully on the uncharted Pitcairn Island. Descendants of the original crew, who took Tahitian women with them as wives, survived until a few years ago on Pitcairn, when the last were forced to leave for lack of food.

The breadfruit is a melon-sized, leathery-skinned fruit that grows on tall trees belonging to the mulberry family. When baked, which is the way breadfruit is usually prepared, it tastes like potato; a creamy, delicious dessert can be spooned from the brown, overripe, uncooked fruit as well. Other recipes call for boiling, frying, roasting or grinding breadfruit in flour that is made into bread.

Banana cutters at work on a plantation in Ecuador.

DATE PALM

Dates have been cultivated in North African and Middle Eastern deserts for at least eight thousand years and are considered by some to be a perfect food. The Muslims call the date the "Tree of Life" because all parts of it are collectively used in over eight hundred different ways. Chemically, dates are a storehouse of iron, sugar, calcium, potassium and vitamins and contain much protein (2.2 per cent) for a fruit. In many Middle Eastern countries children eat dates as natural sweets, which promote growth without causing tooth decay.

The date palm is the familiar palm pictured in drawings of desert oases. New palms are grown from shoots cut from the base of the rough trunk or sometimes from the seeds found within the fruit.

Two-thirds of the world's supply, equal to more than two million tons yearly, is grown in the hot, dry Nile Valley, Tunisia, Algeria and in the oases of the Sahara and Arabian deserts. Some good varieties are also grown in Arizona and California.

Unripe dates are green in color and very bitter. During ripening the color turns brown, red or amber, the flesh becomes soft, and a delightfully sweet aroma develops.

DURIAN

In the Spice Islands, as well as in Malaya and Burma, local inhabitants have enjoyed the durian for centuries. The tall trees that bear durians grow up to eighty feet in height. Within the fruit's tough, thorny-looking exterior lies a foul-smelling but very flavorful and sweet flesh. Alfred Russell Wallace, the great nineteenth-century English naturalist, traveled extensively throughout the Malay archipelago and was one of the first Europeans to describe the flavor of this fruit: "a rich butter-like custard highly flavored with almonds . . . with it comes wafts of flavor that call to mind cream-cheese, onion sauce, brown sherry."

Not only is the durian interesting in taste, it consists of 3 per cent protein, which is the highest protein content of any fruit. Perhaps a large-scale durian-growing operation could supply millions of undernourished people with an inexpensive yet tasty and nutritious food.

LYCHEE

The lychee tree remains a symbol of plenty to many Chinese who love its gelatinous, sweet-fleshed fruit. This favorite fruit of China is an important cultivated crop in India, South Africa and Southeast Asia. Some lychees are also grown and sold as fresh fruit in Florida and California. The tough, brittle, red shell is discarded and the fleshy fruit eaten fresh or dried. The lychee "nuts" sold in Chinese restaurants are white, fleshy fruits, often served in a sweet syrup.

OLIVE

The olive, grown primarily in Spain, Italy, Greece and Turkey, comes from gnarled trees that are an unforgettable sight. Green olives come from the same trees as black ones. If the fruits are picked unripe, they are green. If left on the trees until ripe, they are black. Whether they are picked green or black, olives must be treated with lye and pickled in brine before they are edible. Olives cannot be eaten raw because of the presence of a bitter oil.

The ancient Egyptians, Romans and Greeks extracted oil from olives and made cakes from their pulp after crushing them between stones. The olive is frequently mentioned in the Bible as one of the most useful of all plants. The oil was not only edible but also highly valued as lamp oil.

PAPAYA

Papayas are delicious fruits that are rarely seen in the markets of North America, although canned papaya juice is generally available. Originally native to Mexico or the Caribbean, the papaya is grown today in India, Ceylon, Malaya, Hawaii and the Pacific, as well as in California and Florida.

The seeds are often started in containers, and later the tiny seedlings are transplanted to the field. During its brief two- to three-year life span, the papaya tree bears approximately one hundred green and yellow fruits.

The gnarled trunk of an olive tree is an unforgettable sight

One cooking secret of the tropics is to rub tough meat with the white, sticky juice that comes from the trunk and branches of this tree. Analysis has shown that it contains a powerful protein-digesting enzyme named papain, a substance that is used in commercial meat tenderizers.

Long before great pineapple plantations were established elsewhere, the Indians of northern Paraguay had been growing this fruit for their own consumption. Today Hawaii accounts for about one-third of the world's crop and is followed by Brazil, Puerto Rico, Malaysia, Mexico, Taiwan, the Philippines and South Africa.

PINEAPPLE

The delicious fruit is surrounded by sharp-pointed leaves, and when it is harvested, its crown or tiny suckers are removed for replanting. Although the fruit and its juice are the main object of the efforts of cultivation, by-products are also being utilized. Cattle feed is made from the skin of the pineapple, and the leaf fibers can be manufactured into cloth.

Other Fruit Plants

These are but a few of the more than seven hundred kinds of fruits grown in the tropics and subtropics. Many familiar varieties have been omitted, such as the lemon, lime, grapefruit, orange, tangerine and other citrus fruits. Other widely eaten fruits include the custard apple, fig, guava, jackfruit, kumquat, mango, mangosteen, pomegranate and tamarind.

Fruit—Vegetables

Before leaving the fruits and going to the vegetables, we must look briefly at an intermediate group sometimes called "fruit vegetables." This group includes the eggplant, okra, pumpkin and varieties of squash. Many people think of these as vegetables because they must be cooked thoroughly before they are eaten, but technically they are fruits because they develop from ovaries inside the female plants.

EGGPLANT

The eggplant is native to India and is now grown as a food plant in warm climates, including the United States. These fruits are usually sliced and served fried or boiled.

OKRA

Okra, a native of northeast Africa, has been especially popular in Louisiana since its introduction in the sixteenth century. The fruit is often cooked in stews and soups, called "gumbo," another word for this plant.

SQUASHES

Squashes were an important food of the Indians of North and South America and were usually eaten either baked or boiled. Squashes were often planted with corn and were as highly regarded because of their nutritive value and the fact that they were easily stored after drying, sometimes for months. This ensured a supply of food even through winter, when crops could not be grown.

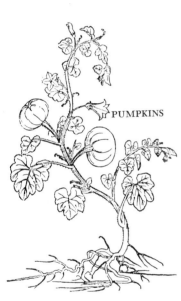

PUMPKINS

Pumpkins, which are a kind of squash, are popular for pie-filling and for carving up into jack-o'-lanterns at Halloween. Other varieties of squash include acorn squashes, crookneck squashes and zucchinis.

VEGETABLES

Technically, all plants are considered vegetables. For the sake of convenience many people usually apply the term to those edible plant parts that are eaten raw, as salad, or with little cooking. Of course, not all edible vegetables conveniently follow this definition. Some, such as the potato, yam, or cassava, require considerable cooking before they are edible. These root crops are underground vegetables that have been described in a previous chapter. Other underground vegetables that have not yet been described are listed in Table 4. Some, such as carrots and radishes, are roots; others, such as the Jerusalem artichoke, are underground stems. Onions, garlics and leeks store their food in bulbs, which is the part eaten by man.

Vegetables that store their nutrients in portions of the plant aboveground in stems, shoots, leaves or flowers are also listed. The following table incorporates all parts of a plant that may be eaten, with the exception of fruits and nuts, which have been treated separately.

In general, underground vegetables have a high water content and large amounts of carbohydrate, usually in the form of starch. Aboveground vegetable parts contain fewer carbohydrates but more proteins, minerals and vitamins, which make them especially valuable in the human diet.

Overleaf: Table 4
Some Edible Vegetables

TABLE 4 *Some Edible Vegetables*

VEGETABLE	PART EATEN GROWS UNDERGROUND			PART EATEN GROWS ABOVEGROUND				NATIVE OF	PRINCIPAL REGIONS OF GROWTH	HOW SERVED
	root	stem	bulb	stem	shoot	leaves	flower			
Artichoke							X (flower head)	Mediterranean	Central and southern Europe, California	Usually steamed or boiled
Asparagus					X			Eastern Mediterranean	Worldwide	Raw or boiled (comparatively rich in protein)
Bamboo					X			Asia	Eastern Asia	Boiled or pickled
Beet	X					X		Southern Europe	Europe, U.S.	Fresh, pickled, boiled, canned; leaves also eaten
Broccoli				X			X	Central Europe (descendant of wild cabbage)	From Arctic to the sub-tropics	Usually briefly steamed or boiled
Brussels sprouts						X (stem buds)		Coastal Europe (descendant of wild cabbage)	Throughout Temperate Zone	Briefly steamed or boiled
Cabbage						X		Coastal Europe (descendant of wild cabbage)	Throughout Temperate Zone	Raw in salads or coleslaw; cooked, as sauerkraut, which originated in Asia (has minerals and is rich in vitamin C)
Carrot	X							Near East	Worldwide	Raw or cooked (rich in vitamin A and sugar)
Cauliflower				X				Coastal Europe (descendant of wild cabbage)	Throughout Temperate Zone	Raw when young, boiled or cooked in various ways
Celery						X (leafstalks)		Temperate Europe	Throughout Temperate Zone	Raw, cooked or in soups
Chives						X		Many regions of Northern	Throughout Northern	Leaves and bulbs used as seasoning

Table 4

Vegetable	Part grows aboveground (stem, shoot, leaf or flower)	Part grows underground (root, stem or bulb)	Native to	Where grown	How used
Collards	X		Coastal Europe (descendant of wild cabbage)	Temperate Zone; much grown in southern U.S.	Boiled
Endive	X		India	Throughout Temperate Zone	Lower leaves eaten raw in salads or as cooked greens
Garlic		X	Southern Asia	Mediterranean, Far East, U.S.	Used as a flavoring or spice, raw or cooked
Horseradish		X	Eastern Europe	Eastern Europe, U.S.	Grated root used as a condiment; fresh or in vinegar
Jerusalem artichoke		X	North America	Northern U.S., Canada	Boiled, baked, pickled or eaten raw
Leeks	X		Southern Asia or Near East	Northern Europe	Boiled, in soups and stews or eaten fresh like onions
Lettuce	X		Southern Europe, Asia	Worldwide	World's most popular fresh salad plant (rich in vitamin A and iron)
Onions		X	Central Asia	Europe, Japan, U.S., U.A.R.	Fresh, cooked, boiled, fried, in soups and stews
Parsley	X		Mediterranean	Many temperate regions	Fresh or dried as a garnish and in cooking many dishes (rich in vitamin C)
Radish		X	Uncertain origin	Worldwide	Raw, in salads; also cooked (contains insulin, a sugar edible by diabetics)
Rhubarb	X (leafstalk)		Asia	Many temperate regions	Leafstalks used in pies and sauces; juice made into wine
Spinach	X		Southwest Asia	In cool places worldwide	Leaves boiled in little water, eaten as greens (rich in proteins and vitamin A)
Turnip		X	Europe	Worldwide	Boiled, baked, in soups and stews; leaves eaten as greens

To read Table 4, find the vegetable in the column on the extreme left and read across until you find an X and you can see whether the vegetable part eaten grows underground and is a root, stem or bulb, or if it grows aboveground and is a stem, shoot, leaf or flower.

SPICES
AND FLAVORS

Spices are not foods in the sense that they contain almost no nutritive value. Used to impart interesting flavors and scents to food, some spices such as hot peppers do affect man physiologically. Nevertheless, spices are neither staple nor accessory foods, as defined on page 10. They are dietary adjuncts which are added to many meals without being essential.

The use of spices developed early in man's history, particularly in the tropics. Heat decomposes food, especially meats, very quickly. By sprinkling spices like pepper or cloves on decaying or tasteless meat, early man managed to disguise the poor taste while improving the flavor and scent. Also, since some spices promote perspiration, which cools the body, they were in particular demand in the tropics. Before air-conditioning was invented, man relied upon other means to keep himself cool.

At the time of the collapse of the Roman Empire, the food in Europe was quite tasteless, especially during the long, cold months of winter. Cattle fodder could not be stored through the freezing weather, and so animals were slaughtered in the fall and their flesh preserved as salted meat. Salt is one of the least harmful of all preservatives, but it can do little in the way of making old meat taste as good as fresh. In those early days even the rich and powerful were unable to get some of the simplest foods now consumed by even the poorest American. There were no potatoes, corn, lemons, sugar, coffee, tea or chocolate. The tastelessness of everyday eating was overwhelming.

A sixteenth-century caravan bringing spices from Asia.

Then by chance Europeans discovered the value of spices. Their demand for pepper, cinnamon and ginger was loud and persistent. A little sprinkle of any of these spices gave the blandest food a more interesting taste. Soon the value of spices equaled that of the precious metals. By the eleventh century pepper was worth its weight in silver. In many towns taxes were paid in peppercorns, and to steal a sack of this coveted spice was to risk one's life.

For centuries the Arabs had controlled the world's spice trade by maintaining a secret trade with the Spice (or Molucca) Islands, a fertile group of volcanic uprisings whose location was then unknown to the Europeans. Eventually Marco Polo found the true location of these fabulous islands. Returning overland through the Orient with tales of seeing pepper under cultivation in India, cloves and nutmegs in the Moluccas, camphor and ginger in China, this explorer further whetted the European appetite for spices.

Soon many major attempts were made to reach the Orient by sea. The merchants who outfitted the expeditions believed they could make great fortunes by filling their ships with spices. It was Vasco da Gama in 1499 who eventually succeeded in returning from the East Indies by sea, by sailing around the Cape of Good Hope in Africa. His cargo from the Molucca Islands consisted of nutmegs, cinnamon, cloves, pepper and ginger.

The discovery of this sea route to the Spice Islands enabled Portugal to monopolize the valuable spice trade for nearly two hundred years. The success of this small country made the great European powers envious. With their enormous profits the Portuguese constructed great churches and buildings, and this period of architecture remains the greatest in that country's history. The economy of Portugal has never returned to the level gained by trading in a few natural products.

Queen Isabella of Spain wanted to take some of the spice trade away from Portugal, and this is why she outfitted Columbus with the three old ships that sailed west and landed unexpectedly in America. Columbus was actually seeking a western route to the lucrative islands of spices, and although he noted that allspice, cocoa and vanilla were growing in the West Indies, he returned with empty holds because these commodities were then unknown in Europe.

By the sixteenth century the Dutch came to dominate the spice trade. Through absolute ruthlessness and the murder of thousands of native laborers, they amassed great fortunes. These fortunes were generously distributed among Dutch poets, musicians, scholars and painters who used the freedom gained by this "blood money" to create some of the greatest masterpieces the world has ever known. For the next two hundred years the Dutch controlled the spice market and maintained their economic world supremacy. In the early eighteenth century the Dutch lost their monopoly to the English, who later lost it to the Americans.

By the late eighteenth century the United States, with an excellent fleet of merchant ships, was trading with every sizable spice-growing country in the tropics. By this time the East Indies were no longer the sole geographic locale of spices and flavorings. Spices had been smuggled from the Indies and planted in many tropical countries. Some of the finest examples of American architecture were constructed during this period with funds gained in the spice trade.

Black pepper is ground from little peppercorns that are the dried unripe fruits of a climbing vine. The pepper vine grows naturally around tree trunks to heights of thirty feet, but under cultivation cuttings are planted in rows at the bases of long stakes. The small peppercorns are hand picked just before they ripen, while still green in color. Within days they turn black, and after some additional drying time they are sent to the marketplace.

The milder white pepper is taken from the inner portion of the same peppercorns after the outer husk has been removed by boiling and fermentation. These additional processes require time and labor, which increase the cost of white pepper. To make white pepper from black peppercorns, soak them in water for about a week and then allow the tiny fruits to ferment by keeping them in a dark place for a few days, stirring them occasionally. After the black outer husks are removed, the white seed inside should be redried and ground to produce powdered white pepper, a favorite in European kitchens.

Our modern-day grocers take their name from the fourteenth-century pepperers who were in charge of weighing shipments of pepper and other spices on their great-beam scales, or *peso gròsso* weights. They were also in charge of sifting and inspecting loads of spices for adulteration or poor quality.

Cleaning black pepper corns by hand in Indonesia.

Red pepper, also known as chili pepper, bell pepper and paprika, is a relative of the tomato plant. These familiar spices, which originated with a plant native to tropical America and the West Indies, have resulted from intensive cultivation since their discovery by Europeans at the time of Columbus. Both the red pepper and the tomato are members of the nightshade family, a group well known for poisonous and medicinal species. Red pepper in its several forms is used to flavor hot dishes like chili con carne, goulash and tamales. The tiny seeds found inside the red fruits of chili pepper are even hotter and sometimes find use in medicine as a stimulant.

The mustard used for flavoring meats and other foods is made from the small seeds of a plant that belongs to the same family as watercress—the mustard family. To manufacture yellow and brown mustards, these small seeds are pulverized and mixed with salt, vinegar and other spices. In addition to imparting flavor to foods, mustard acts as a preservative against the growth of mold in many packaged foods.

This spicy seed was named while Britain was occupied by Rome. Mustard is derived from "must-seeds," a reference to the way in which the seeds were processed—by soaking them in a grape-juice solution then known as "must" solution.

Mustard is one of the few spice plants that is able to grow well outside the tropics. Large quantities of mustard seeds are grown in California and in Montana as far north as the United States–Canadian border.

Ginger is taken directly from rhizomes that have been peeled and dried in the sun. The rhizomes are dug up from cultivated orchards after nine months' growth. Ginger ale and other soft drinks, as well as many baked goods such as gingerbread, owe their snappy flavor to the tall, showy ginger plant. Ginger is also used to make pickles and meat flavorings. Originally from tropical Asia, the ginger plant is now found growing in all tropical countries. Three-fourths of the world's commercial supply comes from India and Taiwan.

Unlike most other spices and flavors, vanilla does not owe its taste to an inherent volatile oil. To prepare commercial vanilla extract, the seed pods of the vanilla orchid are fermented and the flavoring agent within, vanillin, is suspended in alcohol to make it easy to use.

True vanilla is expensive to produce because the orchid is delicate and much hand cultivation is necessary. As a result, imitation vanilla flavoring has gained widespread use. The synthetic flavor is made from a by-product of wood pulp. Pure vanilla extract is still demanded by those who prefer its richer flavor in high-quality ice cream, baked goods and soft drinks.

To make the favorite drink of Montezuma, the ancient Aztec emperor, add one-sixteenth teaspoon pure vanilla extract to your next cup of hot chocolate. The combination of vanilla and chocolate originated in Mexico centuries before the Spanish conquest. Cortez learned of this recipe and brought it back to Europe, where the two flavors became popular at once. The chocolate plant is described in the section on beverages, since cocoa and hot chocolate are two very popular drinks.

CROCUS

The essential ingredient in *arroz con pollo* (rice with chicken) and other Spanish dishes is **saffron**, the world's most expensive spice. More than seventy-five thousand flowers must be picked to produce a pound of saffron. Fortunately, only a tiny pinch added to boiling water imparts the golden color and intriguing flavor that is basic to many Spanish dishes, as well as French bouillabaisse.

The beautiful crocus plant from which saffron is picked is a native of many Mediterranean countries. Spain is the main country of production, but recently many thousands of acres of saffron have been planted in India.

Saffron has been used since ancient times. It was the royal color of Greece and was used by the Romans as a perfume. The spice was in such demand in Germany that during the fifteenth century any spice trader in the city of Nuremburg who mixed other spices into saffron was burned at the stake. An interesting use of this expensive spice may be seen among the Hindus, who apply a spot of the powder to the center of their foreheads.

Cinnamon "sticks" consist of rolled pieces of bark from young cinnamon trees, and ground cinnamon is made by pulverizing the dried bark. Originally native to Ceylon, cinnamon, a member of the laurel family, is now cultivated in India, Burma, the West Indies and South America. Young plants are cut twice a year for their bark, which is carefully peeled and rolled. Cinnamon is popular not only as a cooking spice but as a flavoring for chewing gum, candy, perfumes and soaps.

CINNAMON

Allspice is so named because it imparts a flavor that resembles a mixture of nutmeg, cinnamon and cloves. It is gathered as the green fruit of a small evergreen tree that is grown mainly in Jamaica. After drying for a few days, the green fruits gain their aroma and turn to reddish brown. Allspice is mainly used as a flavoring agent.

ALLSPICE

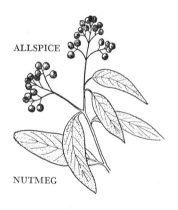

NUTMEG

Nutmeg is the seed of a small evergreen tree native to the Spice Islands. When ripe, the golden yellow fruits of this tree look like small pears or apricots. Stripped of their fleshy coverings, nutmegs are dried and coated with lime to guard against insect infestation. Ground nutmeg is a popular ingredient in puddings, custards, pies and beverages. Surprisingly, in large quantity this spice may have narcotic effects that produce nausea, dizziness and confusion. Added in small amounts to foods and drinks, it remains a highly valued flavoring.

Mace, a membrane that surrounds the seed of nutmeg, is similar to nutmeg, both chemically and in taste, and is especially used to flavor sauces and catsup. To prepare mace for market, the membrane is peeled from the nut, pressed flat and then dried.

The value of spices in the early days of the trade was so great that hand-carved wooden "nutmegs" were often slipped into shipments of real nutmegs to take up space and make the shipments seem larger. In those days a man's labor, even his artistry, was worth less than a few spices found growing wild in nature.

BEVERAGE PLANTS

Man has created many beverages that are enjoyed daily throughout the world. Water still remains the basic drink and is the principal ingredient of all beverages. Very often the "taste" or "flavor" of a beverage rests largely with the water used to make it. Beers in particular owe their flavor characteristics to the water, and some brewers even keep their source of water a trade secret.

Beverages may be conveniently categorized into two two groups: nonalcoholic and alcoholic.

Nonalcoholic beverages include tea, which is used by half the peoples of the world; coffee, which is used by one-third of all the world's people; cocoa, a food and beverage for more than 300 million people; maté, used by more than 15 million South Americans; cola, a popular ingredient of carbonated soft drinks that is also much used in its native Africa; and guaraná, a popular South American beverage. Each of these nonalcoholic beverages is imbibed primarily for the stimulating and refreshing effects of the caffeine they contain.

Alcoholic beverages are formed either as the result of fermentation or distillation. Fermented drinks such as beer, wine and pulque contain relatively little alcohol, while distilled beverages such as strong whiskeys and liqueurs contain much alcohol.

Fruit juices are another widely used group of nonalcoholic beverages, but they are not stimulating drinks (none contain caffeine or any other cerebral stimulant). Soft drinks, or "sodas," are made with carbonated water, sugar and various flavorings. One variety of the cola beverages is discussed in this section.

At least half the people in the world drink "the cup that cheers but not inebriates." The beneficial qualities of tea leaves were discovered in the Orient thousands of years ago quite by accident. It is said that some Buddhist priests, unable to drink the foul water near their temple, steeped in it the leaves of an aromatic shrub that grew in the vicinity, simply to mask the water's unpleasant taste. They so enjoyed the mild stimulating effects that word spread of this experiment, and the shrub was soon cultivated throughout the region.

Of course, there are other stories about the origin of this delightful beverage. None argue that it was in China that tea was first discovered. The Chinese emperor Kien Lung most aptly extolled the virtues of these leaves when on his deathbed he wrote:

> Set a tea-pot over a slow fire; fill it with cold water; boil it long enough to turn a lobster red; pour it on the quantity of tea in a porcelain vessel; allow it to remain on the leaves until the vapor evaporates, then sip it slowly, and all your sorrows will follow the vapor.
>
> Arthur Gray, *The Little Tea Book*

Dutch spice traders first introduced tea to Europe in 1610. Slowly tea became a fashionable but expensive drink. Some of the best kinds then cost as much as fifty dollars a pound. One prominent Dutch physician advised his patients to drink at least eight to ten cups of tea daily, and he even went so far as to claim that he drank fifty, one hundred and sometimes two hundred cups a day.

Not everyone was in favor of this new beverage. As with all new and popular things, there was serious opposition. Some labeled it unfit for civilized people, and others claimed that it was harmful and the source of idleness. In spite of all opposition, however, tea grew in popularity. It became the national drink in England and Russia. The Russian samovar (meaning "to boil itself," from the Greek) is a large brass urn that was devised to keep water boiling throughout the day and night so tea could be prepared at any time. Tea reached New England in 1714. Not only was tea drunk, but the boiled leaves were eaten as a vegetable with salt and butter added.

The quality of tea depends upon how carefully the plants have been grown and at what altitude. Processing also affects the quality. New tea plants are started from seeds planted in containers. They are transplanted when about a foot high, and the picking of leaves begins when the bush is four or five years old. Only the two leaves at the tip of each branch are plucked for the best tea, and this must be done by hand. Although poor-quality teas may contain other leaves and twigs as well, the highest-quality teas contain just the outermost leaves. Tea bushes are pruned back after ten years, and a plant may produce usable leaves for up to forty years.

Processing begins when the harvested leaves are dried and crushed and then spread in cool fermentation sheds. They are later dried with bursts of hot air. After this treatment the leaves develop their aroma and black color. This type of tea is known commercially as black tea, and it is the most popular in the United States because of its strong flavor. The best-known type of black tea is orange pekoe.

Green tea, an unfermented type, is produced by drying the picked leaves, rolling them to break down the tannin-containing cells and redrying them prior to grading, packing and shipping. This is the preferred type of tea in Asia, being somewhat less strongly flavored than black tea. Some important grades of green tea include gunpowder, hyson, and imperial.

Jasmine, a scented tea, is produced by drying the tea leaves together with jasmine flowers. The flowers are later removed, but the tea retains their scent. Jasmine is known as a semi-fermented tea, and it has the flavor of green tea and the color of black tea.

Tea leaves are hand-picked on a plantation in Uganda (top).
Mechanized harvesters on a collective farm in the USSR (bottom).

Tasting samples of coffee in Brazil (top). Coffee beans
are sorted by hand at a plantation in Costa Rica (bottom).

Picking coffee beans in Costa Rica.

Tannin forms about 10 per cent of dry tea leaves. It is similar to the substances used to tan leather and to make black ink. When taken in quantity, tannin interferes with the digestive processes. Steeping tea leaves for a prolonged period of time causes too much tannin to dissolve in the water and makes the tea injurious. This is the reason tea is steeped for only a short time; little of the tannin is extracted into the beverage, while nearly all the aromatic and stimulating properties are.

The stimulant in tea is known as theine. It is almost identical to caffeine, which is present in coffee and cola beverages. These stimulants act by affecting the cerebrum and give the drinker a fresh sense of alertness. Some doctors think that stimulants such as these can be harmful, and they advise that children and people with nervous disorders avoid stimulants completely. An excellent book on the subject is *Coffee and Caffeine* by Rolf Ulrich.

In terms of production, China is the nation that grows the most tea, but it consumes much of it locally. India and Ceylon presently export more tea than any other countries—the bulk of it to Russia, Britain and Australia. In the United States the consumption of tea is relatively low compared to that of coffee. One source states that from 11 to 13 pounds of coffee are consumed annually per capita, as compared to .08 pound of tea.

COFFEE

According to some accounts, coffee was originally introduced to England as a medicine to counter the effects of drunkenness. At the time, in the early 1600's, beer was the king of drinks and taverns were popular in every town and village. Soon the sobering effects of a cup of coffee became well known. By the later part of the century coffee houses had also become very popular, not only for sobering up but also for sitting and talking.

As with tea, this new beverage was denounced by many. The early enemies of coffee were brewers of beer, who stood to lose much business if the drink became too popular, but many other citizens joined them in their assault on coffee. Idleness was said to result from too much coffee drinking, and the coffee houses, which increasingly drew male patrons, were blamed for "businesses disrupted" and "marriages weakened."

Nevertheless, coffee drinking gained in popularity. By 1700 some of the most prominent English writers became the loudest advocates of this beverage. One historian believes that coffee even affected English literature. He argues that before coffee was introduced, in Shakespeare's time, literature was "a flux of tedious words," while after coffee became popular among the writers, "keen . . . finished elegance [was] dominant."

The stimulant in coffee is caffeine. Although coffee and tea are both stimulants, some believe tea is less harmful because it promotes wakefulness without the agitation that accompanies excessive ingestion of coffee.

Coffee originated in the mountains of Ethiopia and was popular among the Arabs for centuries before it was introduced to Europe. From Mocha, an early center of the coffee trade, the plant was exported to India, Ceylon and the East Indies and later to Holland. From there seedlings were eventually brought to South America. Today Brazil grows one-half of the entire world supply. Much coffee is also grown and exported from other countries in South America, Central America, the Caribbean countries, Indonesia and Africa.

The coffee tree if left to itself grows to a height of twenty feet or more, but when cultivated it is kept to a height of eight or ten feet. It has glossy green leaves and white flowers. Its two-seeded fruits are dark purple when ripe. After roasting they become dark brown and develop the characteristic coffee aroma. Each tree bears up to six pounds of coffee "beans" each year, which after roasting and grinding is reduced to only one pound of coffee ready for the pot.

Surprisingly, green coffee contains 14 per cent protein, as well as 7 per cent sugar, 10 to 13 per cent oil, 12 per cent water and 34 per cent cellulose. In Turkey coffee grounds are not discarded but are mixed with sugar and eaten as a nutritious food.

Grown in the tropics, the best-quality coffee is produced by rich, well-drained soils in moist, mountainous climates. Blue Mountain coffee, grown on the island of Jamaica, is considered by many connoisseurs to be the finest variety. Espresso, popular in cafés throughout Europe and now in the United States, refers to the way in which the coffee beans are roasted, not to any particular coffee type. Espresso is dark roasted and when brewed produces a heavy, bitter beverage.

Theobrama, the Latin name for the chocolate plant, means "food of the Gods." Montezuma, the Aztec emperor, so loved the chocolate beverage prepared from the seeds of this small tree that he drank fifty jars of it a day. The royal beverage was flavored with vanilla and other spices, then beaten to a foam and served in gold goblets.

CACAO

During the Spanish occupation of Mexico, bags of cacao beans were a recognized form of currency. The Spaniards spread this fabled product throughout the West Indies and later brought it to Africa and the Orient. Cacao was introduced to Europe about the same time as tea and coffee and at first was considered a great luxury to be enjoyed only by the wealthy.

Cacao trees are often found growing wild beneath larger trees along riverbanks. When cultivated, they are grown directly from seeds planted in the ground. Pods appear on the trunk and lower branches in the fourth year. Inside each of these pods are about forty nutritious and flavorful seeds from which chocolate and cocoa are produced. They contain up to 50 per cent oil, known as cocoa butter, 15 per cent starch, 15 per cent protein, and theobromine, a mild stimulant.

To produce milk chocolate, the beans are fermented, roasted and ground; then sugar, milk, vanilla and extra cocoa butter are added. Cocoa is made by pressing out most of the cocoa butter after roasting the seeds. Chocolate is rich and sweet because it contains cocoa butter and sugar, while cocoa is dry and bitter.

Chocolate is produced and exported mainly by Ghana and Nigeria, and some of the world's commercial crop originates in Brazil and other parts of South America. Tropical regions in Asia and the Pacific countribute a small amount as well.

MATÉ Just as millions of people drink coffee and tea in other parts of the world, millions in South America enjoy maté. The characteristic aromatic flavor and the stimulant caffeine are extracted by pouring water, either hot or cold, over dried leaves. As with tea, the most expensive grade of maté is composed of the youngest leaves, while cheaper grades contain twigs, stems and older leaves. Botanically, maté is a species of holly. It is cultivated and is also found growing wild.

COLA The flavoring for many soft drinks is derived from seeds contained within the pods of the tropical African cola tree. These seeds contain the stimulant caffeine and are sometimes chewed by West African people to allay hunger and fatigue. A native cola drink is made by boiling the pulverized seeds in water for several minutes.

Although the well-known drink Coca-Cola was originally prepared from cola nuts and coca leaves, the highly stimulating coca leaves have been excluded from this beverage since the early part of this century.

GUARANÁ Guaraná is another caffeine-rich beverage of South America. It is made from the pulverized fruits of a vinelike plant that grows wild in the Amazon Valley or is cultivated on small plantations. Sometimes called the "cola of Brazil," guaraná contains two to three times as much caffeine as coffee or tea. This makes it one of the most powerful of all caffeine drinks.

Alcoholic Beverages

Beer and wine, as well as all distilled spirits, are also derived from plants. It is well known that alcohol is a poison that causes bodily damage if consumed in large amounts over a long period of time. Alcoholic beverages are included here because they are consumed throughout the world in large quantities and are important examples of plants that are utilized by man.

Beer is made by fermenting a sweet liquid obtained chiefly from barley malt. Yeast, another plant, is added to convert the sugar into alcohol. Hops [right], a plant of the mulberry family, are added for their bitter flavor. They have a sedative effect that adds to the stupefying action of beer.

BARLEY
YEAST
HOPS

Beer develops its flavor during the difficult art of brewing and afterward, when it is aged in casks for weeks or months. This popular beverage is mainly composed of water and contains about 5 per cent alcohol.

Wine is made from crushed grapes that are later fermented by yeasts found naturally on the skin of the fruit. Commercial wine makers add more yeast to crushed grapes to promote fermentation. Sugars in the grape juice are converted into alcohol, and at just the right stage fermentation is stopped and the wine sealed in closed casks.

GRAPES

As they age, wines develop their characteristic flavors. Generally at least several years are required to age a good wine. Wines contain 10 to 20 per cent alcohol.

Pulqué is made by fermenting the sweep sap of the large century plant. Pulqué is mainly made by individuals and has never been produced on a large commercial scale. It has a low alcoholic content, whereas mescal, a distilled version of pulqué, contains a high percentage of alcohol and is sold commercially in many regions of Mexico.

CENTURY PLANT

Strong **liquors** such as whiskey, brandy, rum and gin are distilled. They contain 40 to 60 per cent alcohol and are particularly dangerous. Whiskey and gin are distilled from a kind of beer that is made from fermented grains such as corn, wheat or rye. Gin is flavored with berries from the juniper tree and other aromatic agents. Brandy is made by distilling wine, and rum is distilled from fermented molasses.

Liqueurs, such as apricot, cherry, and peach brandy or crème de menthe and crème de cacao, are made by adding sugar and flavorings derived from plants to brandylike spirits.

Pure water is said to be man's most perfect drink. Refreshing and healthful, water remains, with air and food, one of the absolute requirements of life.

Then why, we may ask, did man first tamper with water to create beverages? To add interest to his life, perhaps, by creating flavorful drinks or, more likely, to disguise the unpleasant taste of tainted water. By dipping the leaves, berries or roots of an aromatic plant into a quantity of unpleasant water, our distant ancestors managed to make their basic liquid more palatable.

It is unlikely that man altered water—in the sense of creating other beverages out of it—simply to chase away boredom. Primitive people are generally very practical, conserving energy and resources whenever possible. If early man learned to make beverages, he must have had practical reasons. Perhaps a medicinal decoction, or infusion, of plant parts was appealing in scent and taste. Then not only was it recommended for illness; it was sought after by the general population, who always desire a pleasant change from the "normal."

These may be some of the ways in which man's many beverages originated. Whatever pathway of discovery was operational, water was and still remains the basic ingredient of all beverages.

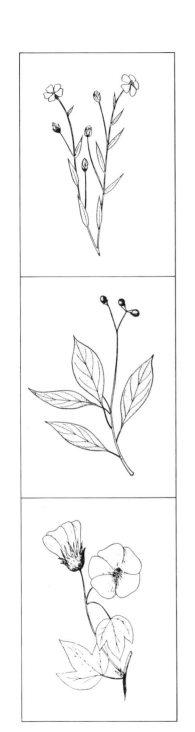

MEDICINES, FABRICS, WOOD, RUBBER AND OTHER PLANT PRODUCTS

Ye who would pass by and raise your hand against me, harken ere you harm me. I am the heat of your hearth on the cold winter nights; the friendly shade screening you from the summer sun; and my fruits are refreshing draughts quenching your thirst as you journey on. I am the beam that holds your house, the board of your table, the bed on which you lie, and the timber that builds your boat. I am the handle of your hoe, the door of your homestead, the wood of your cradle, and the shell of your coffin. I am the gift of God and friend of man.

From a sign at a public park in Portugal

The unknown author of these words certainly carried the proper respect for his plant allies. He recognized the value of trees but could have added: "I am the medicine at your sick bed, the friendly scents that please you, the leaves you smoke contentedly, the paper that you write on. I am the rubber that your vehicles roll on, the polish on your floors, the colors on your artists' brushes, the clothes and ropes you spin."

Not all useful plant products come from trees alone. Some originate with tiny microflora; others come from beneath the sea, from mushrooms on the forest floor, as well as lichens on the arctic rocks. In this section some of man's useful plants other than foods and beverages will be described.

MEDICINES, ARROW POISONS, INSECTICIDES AND PERFUMES

MEDICINES

While the abuse of drugs may be a particularly nonproductive characteristic of contemporary Western society, most societies have been drug oriented since early times. Primitives and moderns alike have used medicines to lessen pain, to heal wounds and to treat illnesses, while many people have used plant drugs to escape occasionally from reality.

In early societies people who had the abilities to determine which herb was good medicine became doctors. Those who specialized in learning which mixture of substances could kill became witch doctors, feared by all and consulted by anyone wishing to dispose of an enemy or to appease an "evil" spirit. Primitive medicine was often surrounded by elaborate ceremonies with chanting priests, and often an entire tribe was brought to the bedside of a sick person. This made it difficult to know whether a cure was the result of a particular drug plant or the power of these other influences as well.

Slowly man's knowledge of the curing properties of plants evolved. By experimenting with herbs to cure particular ailments, men began to discover which remedies actually worked. By the nineteenth century scientific chemistry was sufficiently well established to appraise many herbs that were well known for their curative properties. Many different leaves, roots, bark and berries were passed through flames, subjected to harsh acids and tested on animals.

New reports of herbal remedies continued to flow back to the chemist's bench. It was said that the American Indians were able to lower fevers by drinking an infusion of the bark of willow trees. South American Indians were said to have another, if not even more effective, bark medicine for high fevers. The French were astounded to learn that the explorer Cartier and his men had been cured of scurvy by drinking an infusion of the bright green needles of black spruce—a secret given to them by a tribe of Canadian Indians.

Through the nineteenth century and into the twentieth, these drug plants and thousands more were subjected to critical tests. As a result, man has developed a tremendously effective array of medicines, poisons and insect killers.

Although the present trend is toward the development of synthetic drugs from nonplant sources, over 37 per cent of all prescriptions written in the United States still call for drugs made from plants. The average physician in the United States writes about eight plant-derived prescriptions daily.

Antibiotics are the largest category of prescription drugs in the United States. Over two hundred types of antibiotics have been discovered, and of these the most frequently prescribed are tetracycline, neomycin, erythromycin, and penicillin.

Penicillin was discovered by Sir Alexander Fleming in an accidental way. In 1928 Dr. Fleming was culturing dangerous disease-causing bacteria under glass covers in special culturing dishes. One morning he returned to his laboratory to find that his cleaning lady had opened some of these culture plates to the air. Fleming was about to discard the "spoiled" bacterial cultures when he noticed a green mold growing on the surface. What was unusual was that the original colony of disease-causing bacteria was much reduced in size. Fleming concluded that the contaminating green mold was responsible for destroying the dangerous bacteria. On examining the strange mold he found it to be *Penicillium notatum*, the same green mold that often grows on old bread. Oddly enough, centuries earlier the wounds of many European soldiers were often treated with pieces of moldy bread. Here is a fine example of a folk remedy that later proved to be a truly effective medicine.

Penicillin was not developed commercially from these green molds until World War II, when the need for new drugs was greatly increased. In 1944 another antibiotic, streptomycin, was discovered. Today these antibiotics are normally developed from living microorganisms in special vats. Selected microbes are submerged in special chemical solutions and allowed to grow and produce the desired antibiotics.

As a result of the development of antibiotic drugs from microbes, diseases such as tuberculosis, dysentery, pneumonia, tetanus, typhoid fever and diphtheria are now treatable if diagnosed in early stages.

These "against life" (*anti+biotic*) drugs are sometimes harmful. They can dissolve and destroy beneficial organisms in the body, and prolonged dependence on them weakens the natural bodily defenses against disease organisms. Nevertheless, many of us owe our lives to these simple plants and the people who discovered how they work.

The microorganisms that give us many useful antibiotic drugs belong to an important group of simple plants that are also the source of many enzymes, vitamins and immunizing agents. These tiny plants play the key role in microbiological work and are frequently utilized in the production of organic compounds. As the writer Robert de Ropp has noted, "The humblest bacterium can synthesize, in the course of its brief existence, more organic compounds than can all of the world's chemists combined."

WILD YAM

Next to antibiotics, **steroid drugs** derived from wild yam plants account for the second largest category of drugs used in the United States. These drugs include birth-control pills, male and female sex hormones and cortisone.

Derived initially from the glands of animals, sex hormones in the early 1940's cost about two hundred dollars per gram (1/28 oz.). At that time it required the ovaries of eighty thousand female pigs to produce 12 *milligrams* of a female sex hormone—quite an expensive production.

Because of the terribly high costs of producing hormones from animal glands, chemists looked for cheaper sources. They soon discovered that it would be less costly to create steroid hormones from similar compounds existing in a few known species of plants. These "starter" plant compounds are known as sapogenins. Expeditions to Africa in search of sapogenin-rich plants proved disappointing. Large quantities of the desired seeds could not be obtained.

Eventually a chemistry professor, Russell E. Marker, managed to locate sapogenin-rich wild yam plants in Mexico. He established a chemical company and by himself produced four and one-half pounds (1916 grams) of progesterone, the pregnancy hormone. This quantity was then worth $150,000. By placing it on the open market, Marker drove the high price of sex hormones down to half the former cost.

As a result, these drugs and others created from steroid "starter" compounds in yams have become available to the millions of people who need them. Today birth-control pills, which are produced from material in the yam plants native to Mexico, account for over $60 million in foreign exchange for that country.

Cortisone is another valuable steroid drug that is made from compounds in yams. It is used in treating many painful diseases such as arthritis and rheumatism, as well as bronchial asthma, certain skin diseases and brain disorders.

Pain is one of the most frequent medical complaints. **Pain-relieving drugs** are the fourth most prescribed category of plant medicines, and of all natural pain relievers morphine is the most frequently employed. This drug is chemically extracted from opium, which comes from the opium poppy.

Egyptian hieroglyphics and early Greek and Roman legends tell of the pain-relieving properties of the poppy plant. Morphine is aptly named for Morpheus, the son of sleep and the god of dreams. This sleep-inducing drug is highly addictive. As is well known, most of the world's opium crop finds its way into illegal trade. Both morphine and heroin—a dangerous, highly addictive derivative—are presently sold at enormous profits at the expense of millions of addicts.

Fields of this spiny-leaved herb are cultivated in India, China, Southeast Asia, the Near East and in many Mediterranean countries. The plants have large, showy flowers and are often grown as ornamentals. Some are occasionally found growing in the United States.

When cultivated, the plants are grown from tiny seeds planted directly in the fields. These seeds are the familiar poppy seeds found on "seeded" rolls and other baked goods. They are not dangerous because they do not contain any of the narcotics present in opium. Secondly, they have been baked at high heat and sterilized so that they will not yield seedlings if planted.

A few months after planting, the poppy plants produce flowers and several seed capsules. At sunset, when it is cool, workers go through the fields with special cutting tools to scratch the ripe capsules. A whitish substance appears on the surface and is allowed to harden overnight.

The next morning the sticky dried latex is scraped from the capsules and rolled into brownish balls of crude opium. From this crude opium, morphine and codeine are made for legitimate medical use. Both drugs are widely prescribed for their pain- and cough-inhibiting properties.

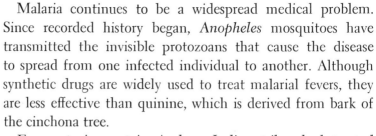

Malaria continues to be a widespread medical problem. Since recorded history began, *Anopheles* mosquitoes have transmitted the invisible protozoans that cause the disease to spread from one infected individual to another. Although synthetic drugs are widely used to treat malarial fevers, they are less effective than quinine, which is derived from bark of the cinchona tree.

For centuries certain Andean Indian tribes had treated the high fevers of malaria by boiling the bark of cinchona and drinking the liquid. The Indians shared their secret medicine with missionaries and occasional Europeans who suffered from the horribly painful fevers. As a result, a small group of Europeans established trade in this bark, demanding and receiving high prices on the world market.

To secure their own source of the "fever bark," the British authorized an expedition to the Andes in 1860. With the help of a friendly Indian, the British managed to secure some seedlings and seeds of the valuable cinchona tree. The helpful Indian was later jailed and beaten to death by those Europeans in Bolivia who wished to maintain their control over the high prices paid for the valuable bark.

The British could now grow cinchona trees on plantations in India, Ceylon and Burma. Soon trees were developed that yielded higher quantities of quinine than those found in the wilds of the Andes. The price of this valuable drug fell remarkably, and quinine became available to even the poorest sufferer in tropical regions around the world.

Under cultivation cinchona trees are grown from seed and later grafted with buds from specially grown varieties that produce much quinine in their bark. After seven years these evergreen trees with bright, shiny leaves are cut down and the bark removed from the trunk, root and branches. After drying in the sun, the bark is shipped to drug factories where quinine is removed by treating the bark with solvents. Although most quinine is used as medicine, a small amount goes into the manufacture of a flavoring for tonic drinks.

Digitalis, a frequently prescribed heart medicine, comes from one of the most attractive of all European wildflowers, the foxglove. Mentioned in many early books of herbal medicine, foxglove leaves are known to strengthen the heartbeat while slowing the pulse.

FOXGLOVE

Although all the digitalis that is presently required for medical purposes could be made from the wild stands of foxglove growing in Europe, a few hundred acres of it are grown in Holland to make collection a simpler task and to reduce overall production costs.

Other Plant Medicines

Other significant drug plants include the belladonna plant, which is cultivated for the atropine in its leaves, used as an antidote for opium poisoning and as a muscle relaxant. The rauwolfia plant is famous for the drug reserpine made from it, used to lower blood pressure. This plant medicine originated in the folk medicine of India and is today used in many prescription drugs throughout the world.

BELLADONNA
RAUWOLFIA

Additional drug plants include the laxatives derived from cascara plants; the amoeba-killing ipecac herb; the migraine-relieving ergot fungus that is commonly found on spoiled rye grains; and colchicine from the autumn crocus, one of the only treatments for gout.

CASCARA
IPECAC HERB
ERGOT FUNGUS
AUTUMN CROCUS

There is also a broad range of hallucinogenic drugs that some scientists think may prove useful in certain psychiatric disorders. These drugs have been culled from primitive tribes around the globe and include peyote, widely used by certain Indian tribes in the southwestern United States, virola and caapi of South America; marijuana of Asian origin; and the fly agaric mushroom of Siberia that was used by native priests when seeking "divine" insights.

PEYOTE
VIROLA
CAAPI
MARIJUANA
FLY AGARIC

There are hundreds, if not thousands, of other plant drugs in use throughout the world, both in "official" medicine and in native cures. Who can say which of these might become the leading drug of tomorrow?

ARROW POISONS

In the early 1940's Dr. Richard Evans Schultes, a botanist from Harvard University, went to the Amazon in search of the mysterious arrow poison, **curare**. The scientist spent thirteen years in South America exploring for this deadly substance, as well as for new medicines and other products of the plant world.

Today Dr. Schultes is director of the Botanical Museum of Harvard University. According to him, curare was the first of the wonder drugs that have been developed in the past thirty-five years. From this "death-dealing substance made by primitive peoples" scientists have made "life-saving drugs."

Curare arrow poisons are made from crude infusions of the bark of vines found growing on large trees of the tropical rain forest. Tropical Indians have used "the flying death" for centuries, sometimes in warfare but mainly for hunting. Dr. Schultes describes how the ten- to fifteen-foot-long blowguns are used to shoot curare-tipped darts with remarkable accuracy at monkeys in trees as high as 150 feet. If a hunter misses his target, the animals are undisturbed because the dart silently passes them by. When guns are used, the noise usually drives all the animals away.

When a dart hits its mark, the animal is not killed instantly. The poison takes a few minutes to act. By blocking nerve impulses, it causes the monkey or other animal to lose control of its muscles, and the animal falls to the jungle floor below. This muscle-relaxing quality is precisely the reason curare was first used in medicine.

Curare was found to be the only drug that was capable

A Yalma Indian of the Upper Amazon River
hunting with a poison blowgun.

of relaxing dangerously stiffened muscles during deep abdominal surgery. Because it occasionally interfered with respiration, it has since been replaced by synthetic imitations that are more readily controlled. Nevertheless, the curarelike muscle relaxants of modern medicine all owe their creation to those who discovered the silent poison arrows of the Amazon.

There are other arrow poisons as well. Dr. Schultes points out that "hunting with poison darts and arrows is a very ancient culture trait in all continents." Although these poisons are sometimes taken from animals, the majority come from plants.

UPAS TREE
In India and the Malay archipelago the milky latex of the upas tree, a member of the mulberry family, is used to kill. This poison was once used by natives of Malaysia against invading Portuguese soldiers. Even though the foreign soldiers were armed with guns, the local army successfully routed them with their poison-tipped arrows. The Upas poisons are named *antiarin a* and *b*. They act by breaking down the red blood cells and thereby cause death by asphyxiation.

STROPHANTHUS
In Africa the arrow poison *kombe* was found to be made from a strophanthus vine, a member of the dogbane family. From this poison a drug with digitalis-like effects was developed which finds use in some emergency heart problems.

CALABAR BEANS
Dr. Schultes also describes how the drug physostigmine, which comes from calabar beans of African vines, was developed by studying the effects of certain "ordeal poisons" of Madagascar. Individuals accused of crimes were forced to eat the beans. Those who survived the ordeal were thought to be innocent, while those who died were said to be guilty. Oddly enough, physostigmine is the only known antidote for curare arrow poisons. It tenses muscles and is used in medicine to treat myasthenia gravis, a disease characterized by tiredness and painfully relaxed muscles of the neck, legs and jaws.

INSECTICIDES

In an age when insects have developed immunities to formerly effective insecticides and have generally been increasing their numbers on planet earth, technological man has had to look to his technologically undeveloped cousins for new weapons against these pests.

Natural insecticides from the plant world have been discovered by studying the activities of primitive people as well as by experimentally evaluating the effectiveness of hundreds of plant species. Thus far, at least twelve hundred plant species have been found that have some effect against insects. Not all of them are very powerful, nor could they be applied on a wide scale. However, with modification some of these plants may become the only insecticides that are not toxic to higher organisms, including man.

Two groups of plant insecticides that are presently being used include the rotenones and the pyrethrums.

For centuries people in tropical Asia and South America TUBA have used the roots of the rotenone-containing plants tuba BARBASCO (in Asia) and barbasco (in South America). The shredded roots of these plants are used in these regions as fish poisons and not for killing insects. The roots are pounded, then sprinkled in streams or sheltered lagoons to stupefy fish, thereby bringing them to the surface where waiting fishermen gather them in nets. The fish are not rendered poisonous, merely unconscious, and the rotenone is harmless to human beings.

For the past thirty years or so, rotenone in powdered or liquid form has been sprinkled or sprayed on crops with great success. It kills houseflies, mosquitoes, pea aphids, corn borers and bean beetles, as well as pet pests such as fleas, ticks and lice without endangering the pet or other mammals.

The use of rotenone insecticides is increasing greatly since DDT has been shown to be a hazard to many organisms, including man. As man learns to value his own safety and continues to wage a tough battle against extremely well-adapted foes, he will rely even more strongly on rotenone-containing plants.

CHRYSANTHEMUM

The daisylike flowers of a type of chrysanthemum yield another weapon in the battle against insect pests. Pyrethrum insecticides are obtained from the dried flowers of these plants after they have been harvested in such countries as Africa, Japan and New Guinea.

Presently used in powders and sprays, pyrethrums are especially known for their "knock-down" power that paralyzes insects and brings them down within the range of a final blow. Pyrethrum insecticides will never be useful as crop sprays because they lack actual killing power. They remain an amazingly safe, yet effective local insecticide that is particularly useful against flies, fleas, mosquitoes, body lice and other house pests.

PERFUMES AND OTHER VOLATILE OILS

Like many medicines and insecticides, perfumes owe their aromatic scents to the presence of volatile oils. These oils are characterized by the fact that they escape into the atmosphere on contact with the air and generate strong, generally pleasant and invigorating aromas. It is because of this escaping quality that we are able to detect the scent of perfumes and many medicines.

Volatile oils are not to be confused with fatty oils such as are contained in olives, coconuts, soybeans or sunflower seeds. Fatty oils are sometimes known as "fixed" oils because they are fixed inside plant cells and are unable to escape into the atmosphere.

Since ancient times men and women have harvested many plants solely for their intriguing scents. Although synthetic perfume oils are now used in greater quantity than the natural plant-derived perfume oils, the natural oils are still used in producing the better perfumes, primarily because their scents last longer than the artificial oils.

Some of the important perfume oils of plant origin are shown in the following chart. Also listed are the plant parts the perfumes are derived from, the principal regions of cultivation, and the main uses of each perfume oil.

T A B L E 5 Some Perfume Oils

PERFUME OIL	PLANT SOURCES	PRINCIPAL REGIONS OF CULTIVATION	USES
Rose oil	Damask rose—flowers	Bulgaria	Expensive perfumes; rose water
Geranium oil	Geranium—leaves	Algeria, southern France, Spain	Soaps and perfumes; also as a substitute for the more valuable rose oil
Cananga oil	Ylang-ylang tree—flowers	Far East	One of the most expensive plant oils; used in blending many perfumes
Jasmine oil	Jasmine—flowers	Southern France, India	Perfumes
Patchouli oil	Patchouli shrub—leaves and young buds	Indonesia, China	In soaps, hair tonics and to create heavy-scented perfumes; also to flavor tobaccos
Orange-blossom oil (neroli oil)	Bitter orange—flowers	Southern France, Italy, Spain, Portugal	Synthetic perfume
Lemon-grass oil	Lemon grass—leaves	Guatemala, Honduras, India	To scent soaps, cosmetics, mosquito repellents and medicines; derivative used in the synthesis of vitamin A
Citronella oil	Citronella grass—leaves	Java, Ceylon	To scent inexpensive soaps and perfumes; to make menthol

Perfumes and other volatile oils are extracted from plants by distillation. On a simple scale this process consists of boiling the aromatic plant in water until the scent of the perfume oil escapes into the atmosphere with the steam. Since this scent must be "captured" before it can be bottled, commercial distillers use condensers to trap the steam, which contains the perfume oil. After cooling, the perfume oils are removed in filters.

Those perfume oils too delicate to be collected by steam distillation (because steam destroys the perfume) are removed by solvents. Other perfume oils, such as those contained in oranges and lemons, are removed by applying mechanical pressure—in effect, squeezing the oils out of the rinds.

CAMPHOR

In addition to providing us with perfumes, many volatile plant oils find use in industry. Camphor, primarily known in the form of hard, white masses, is extracted by distillation from the wood of the camphor tree, a native of China. Although most commercial camphor is presently synthesized, natural camphor is still a significant cash crop in Taiwan.

PINE TREES

Turpentine, another volatile oil, is derived by steam distillation of various pine trees. Most of this volatile oil goes into the manufacture of synthetic pine oil, which is used in the production of insecticides.

WITCH HAZEL

WORMWOOD

EASTERN RED CEDAR

The liniment witch hazel is distilled from the twigs of a tree by that name [left], which is native to the eastern United States. The wormwood herb yields another volatile oil, known as wormwood, which is also used for liniments as well as for producing the liqueur absinthe; and the eastern red cedar yields cedarwood oil, much used as a moth repellent and as a constituent of many soaps, deodorants, perfumes and polishes.

TOBACCO AND
OTHER STIMULANTS

The stimulating beverages tea, coffee, cocoa, maté, guaraná and cola are consumed daily by hundreds of millions of people. Tobacco leaves, coca leaves and betel nuts are three other widely used stimulants that come directly from plants. They are grouped separately from the beverages because tobacco is smoked, snuffed or chewed, while coca and betel nuts are chewed.

It may be difficult to see why a plant such as tobacco, which is thought to be responsible for serious respiratory illness, is included in a book about "useful" plants. It must be remembered that plants, like man, are organisms that developed through millions of years according to the laws of nature and without specific purpose. How these organisms are used depends upon the chance experimentation of man. Perhaps there are thousands of valuable plants whose uses are yet to be discovered. If a powerful poison were found in one of these plants, would we call it an evil plant? Obviously not. The applications to which any invention or natural substance is applied are a reflection on those who use it. Those who make the decision to use these products are by choice also making themselves responsible for the consequences.

TOBACCO

"A custom loathsome to the eye, hateful to the nose, harmful to the brain, dangerous to the lungs." So wrote King James I of England during the 1600's as smoking was gaining a hold on his people. Many have tried to stop this habit since that time but without much success.

The word *tobacco* is derived from *taboca*, the name of a hollow y-shaped tube that was used by the early inhabitants of the West Indies to snuff dried, ground tobacco leaves. On seeing this custom, Spanish explorers mistakenly applied the name to the ground leaves and spelled it *tabaco*. They brought the leaf back to Europe, and the popularity of tobacco continues to spread around the world despite evidence that smoking is harmful.

Although many varieties of tobacco plants have been developed, all growers start their plantings in seedbeds and later transplant them to the fields. This is necessary because, of the 200,000 tiny weeds produced by each plant, only a few would yield new plants if left to themselves. The seeds are not very hardy because of intensive cultivation. Sometimes artificial selection (instead of natural selection) weakens an organism and lessens its chance for survival.

In most countries tobacco leaves are harvested by removing them from the plants as they mature. They are hung in bunches to "cure," usually in ventilated storage areas but also under forced hot-air heat. In some remote places they are simply dried in the sun. After this initial process of fermentation by drying, leaves of similar quality are sorted together and the bunches sold at auction.

After purchasing the bunches of leaves, manufacturers of cigarettes, cigars and pipe tobaccos store them in large warehouses where a second fermentation takes place during a period lasting up to four years.

Originally cultivated by the Indians of America, the once tropical tobacco plant has many strains that are presently grown in Asia, India, China, Japan, Indonesia, Oceania, Africa, Europe and South America. The United States is the chief producer, followed by China and India and then by Brazil, Japan, the Soviet Union, Turkey, Greece and Rhodesia. Cuban tobacco is regarded as the finest for cigars.

Some consider nicotine, the active principal of tobacco, to be a narcotic because of its apparently soothing effect on

Hanging tobacco leaves to dry in Greece.

A tobacco auction in North Carolina.

the nerves. Most smokers need increasing doses of this drug to "calm their nerves" because they are addicted to it. Despite popular notions about the effects of tobacco, physiologically it has marked stimulating effects on the human system. Unfortunately, nicotine also happens to be a very potent poison. One drop of pure nicotine can kill a dog. At the turn of this century a physician reported that an eight-year-old child died after the juice of fresh tobacco leaves was squeezed on his scalp. Also, during World War II powdered tobacco leaves became one of the most effective of insecticides.

Leaves from the coca shrub, the "divine plant of the Incas," were once reserved for royal families, but today they are chewed by approximately eight million people, the majority of them in three regions of South America. Archaeological evidence indicates that coca leaves have been chewed since 500 B.C. in Peru. COCA LEAVES

The small leaves are mixed with lime from plant ashes and chewed to alleviate hunger and stimulate physical activity. Dr. Richard Schultes, who has spent many years among South American coca chewers, has written that chewing the leaves for their stimulant properties is not addictive and is less harmful than using tobacco or alcohol.

This plant received a bad name because the dangerously addictive alkaloid cocaine is also extracted from the leaves. This, however, is not a native practice. Cocaine is a highly effective anesthetic that has very limited medical uses. A small amount of a weak solution of cocaine dripped on the eye will enable a surgeon to operate on the eye without causing the patient any pain. Cocaine is sometimes used illegally by individuals who inhale it for its stimulant and euphoric effects. The drug is highly addictive and often causes delusions.

It must be remembered that coca leaves contain about fifteen alkaloids in addition to cocaine. In combination these constituents may alter one another's effects. To conclude that chewing the leaves is the same as sniffing or injecting pure cocaine is a mistake that many politicians and law-enforcement officials still make.

Unknown in the wild, coca is today cultivated primarily for local consumption in South America. In Java the crop is grown for international sale to drug companies. The plant is a small shrub or tree, four to seven feet tall, with oval leaves and small white flowers. The leaves are very striking, each having the shape of another leaf within itself.

Seedlings are started in a nursery and transplanted to fields after eight to ten months. When the plants are mature, the leaves are hand picked and dried, either in special sheds or in the sun.

To prepare the leaves for use, the Amazon Indians toast them and then pulverize them in a stone mortar, adding the ashes of the burned leaves of another tree. They then blow this mixture into their mouths through a hollow bone attached to a small sack.

Although coca leaves in pure form were once included in cola drinks, they now have their cocaine alkaloid removed and merely add flavor to these beverages.

BETEL PALM

BETEL PEPPER

The practice of chewing the seeds of the betel palm for their mildly stimulating effects is an ancient custom in southern Asia and the southwest Pacific. Throughout these areas chewing betel nuts is considered to be highly beneficial because it is believed to sweeten the breath, remove food particles from the teeth, maintain strong gums, give the user a "boost" and allay hunger. Many Western observers have described this custom as disgusting because the saliva turns red and is continuously expectorated. Actually this custom differs little from tobacco chewing.

The most popular stimulant for 200 million people consists of betel nuts, lime and other flavorings all wrapped together in the leaf of the betel pepper vine. The lump is chewed without swallowing until the mass is pulverized.

Although many betel chewers have poor teeth, this chewing combination is no longer blamed for the problem. Nutritional deficiencies and the practice of adding a shiny black stain to filed teeth seem to be responsible for widespread dental problems among Philippine chewers, at least. In any case, the ancient custom of chewing betel nuts is not likely to disappear while it remains an important part of so many complex cultures.

A farm worker picking cotton in Israel.

ROPES AND FABRICS FROM PLANT FIBERS

Early man first looked at the surrounding vegetation for food. His next use of plants must have been for fibers with which to fasten together his weapons and tools. He also found that plants could fill his need for clothing. The skins, hair and fur of animals probably supplied the earliest need for warm clothing, but eventually man discovered that many plants contained useful strands supporting stems, roots, leaves and seeds. By removing these strands and twisting or weaving them, he was able to create clothing, bowstrings, fish nets, lines and sails to meet his many needs.

Plant parts continue to provide important fibers that are spun or twisted into yarns, threads and cords. These are woven, braided, knit or netted into fabrics that can be made into clothing, upholstery, curtains, awnings, hammocks, nets, bags or sails.

Today synthetic fibers are widely used and have certain superior characteristics, such as greater strength or the ability to hold their shape longer (in the form of permanent-press fabrics). In the long run, however, vegetable fibers will continue to remain important to man because of their continued availability from plants at low cost, without the need of an industrial city for their creation.

Useful vegetable fibers may come from seeds, as do cotton and kapok; from stems, as do flax, jute and hemp; or from leaves, as do abaca and sisal. Some limited use of the bark of plants for fiber is seen in the South Pacific, where the paper mulberry tree provides the raw material for the highly decorative tapa cloth.

The most useful and valuable of all plant fibers are the white hairs that surround the seeds of the cotton plant. These hairs enable cottonseeds to be carried by the wind. By being spread over a wide area by the wind, the seeds give the species a greater chance for survival.

When cotton is grown under cultivation, the seeds never reach the wind for dispersal. Rather, they are picked as soon as the bolls that hold them ripen and open up. The white cotton is separated from the seeds by a cotton gin, a machine that draws the fine 1 to 1-½-inch-long seed hairs through openings too narrow for the seeds, which are left behind.

The drawn cotton fibers are then combed by machine and spun together into long thin threads or woven into sheets of cloth. Fluffy, white, absorbent cotton, which is nearly pure cellulose, is produced by removing the natural water-repellent film found on raw cotton fibers. Some fine paper is made from cotton rags and fibers too short for spinning. More of the world's clothing is made from cotton than all other plant fibers combined.

Originally introduced to Europe by the Arabs, the cotton plant was brought to America and the West Indies in the early 1600's. In America the Indians had been using a native cotton for centuries before the European variety was introduced.

The cotton-growing industry in the southern United States was an important factor in the darkest period in the history of this country. Africans were captured and forced into slave ships, mainly by Arab slave profiteers, and transported across the Atlantic Ocean to spend their lives in humiliation and defeat.

With the end of the Civil War slavery was abolished. At this point the soil in the cotton regions was exhausted because it had been treated as carelessly as the slaves. Growing this single crop season after season had depleted the soil of the minerals utilized by the cotton plant. The soil eventually became mineral deficient and unable to support cotton or

A large textile mill in El Salvador.

any other crop. As a result, the cotton industry was shifted to the highly fertile soils of the western United States.

Today the leading cotton-producing countries are the United States, the Soviet Union, India, Mexico, Egypt and Brazil.

SEA ISLAND COTTON

Sea island cotton has stronger, softer and longer fibers than the related upland cotton, but its production is quite limited because of the low yields per acre. At one time this fiber was extensively grown on the islands off the coast of the Carolinas and Georgia.

Although cotton is presently the most widely used of all plant fibers, it is not inherently superior to the other fibers. Cotton is more widely used because it is easier to process mechanically than the others and thus cheaper to produce.

FLAX

The finest linen fabrics and the strongest thread come from the flax plant. Linen rags are used to make the finest writing and drawing paper. "Vegetable parchment," popularly used for copies of the Declaration of Independence and the U.S. Constitution, is also made from linen derived from flax.

While flax is of superior quality compared with cotton, its preparation requires more hand labor and so it is more expensive to convert into fabric. Even today most flax is harvested by workmen who must pull it out of the soil by the roots. As a result flax is the second, rather than the first, most important fiber in the world.

After drying in upright stacks, the harvested stems are retted by soaking in streams or water tanks. This process partially rots the stems and makes it easier to free the internal fibers from the gums that bind them to the inner wood of the stems. The partially rotted stems are passed through machines that crush them. A combing process then separates the fractured plant parts from the long, straight, useful fibers. After the longest and toughest fibers have been bleached, they are ready for the weaver.

Flax has been cultivated since prehistoric times. The Swiss lake dwellers who lived during the time of the now extinct mammoth are known to have used flax for making fiber and fabrics. The Egyptians used linen to wrap mummies and also to weave handsome embroideries.

Flax is principally grown in the Soviet Union, the United States, Canada and countries of northern Europe. Ireland, famous for its linen products, was once a large producer but now must import such flax.

One variety of the flax plant contains seeds that are highly valued for their linseed oil. This quick-drying oil is used in the manufacture of putty, varnish and lacquer. The crushed seeds that remain after the oil has been pressed out are formed into oil cakes that are highly valued as cattle feed. Linoleum (from *linum*, flax, and *oleum*, oil) is made by combining linseed oil in layers on a mat of felt or burlap to which resins, gums and powdered cork are added. This material is then baked in ovens for several days to produce a tough, glossy flooring.

Marijuana, a common roadside weed throughout many southern and midwestern states, was introduced to this country by the early settlers as a fiber plant. At that time it was highly valued for making cloth, ropes and sails, as well as for oakum—caulking that was stuffed between the boards of ships to waterproof the hulls.

Hemp is a stem fiber that is cut, dried, retted and crushed like flax. It is stronger and more durable than flax but less elastic and lends itself better to being woven into stiff, tough ropes, twines, threads and canvases.

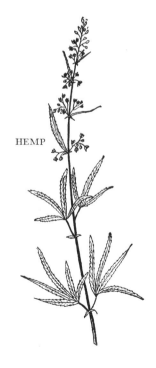

HEMP

Hemp is grown from oil-rich seeds that are also used as bird feed. The plant will grow in cold as well as warm climates and was once grown in most regions of the United States. Some hemp is still grown in this country, but laws govern the exact amount of acreage and areas where it may be cultivated. The Soviet Union is currently the world's lead-

Cutting sisal leaves in El Salvador (top left). Sisal fibers are removed from the plant and dried in the sun in Sudan (bottom left). Making a thatch roof from Motacú palm in Bolivia (below).

ing hemp grower. Large quantities are also grown in China, where it is a significant fiber plant.

ABACA   Abaca (Manila hemp) resembles the banana plant and is grown mainly in the Philippines, where especially tough ropes resistant to salt water are made from its soft, white leaf fibers. During World War II the navy needed abaca to manufacture tough, waterproof ropes. As a result, this valuable fiber was cultivated on a mass scale in 1942 in Central America to increase production and create an independent supply. The plants were grown from seedlings and cuttings that had been smuggled out of the Philippines years before the Japanese military occupied these islands.

To remove the strong fibers, the leaf stalks are cut off at their bases and cut open lengthwise. The strands of fiber are separated from the pulpy plant material, then washed and dried. This was formerly done by hand, but now the fiber is removed and processed by mechanical equipment.

SISAL   Sisal plants are a species of *Agave* and are related to the century plant of the American deserts. They are grown in desertlike regions of Mexico, Africa and Brazil. Their tough, swordlike leaves are crushed by machinery and then scraped by hand with a knife to remove the hard straight fibers. These fibers are mainly used to manufacture twine.

Other Fibers

These few species are by no means all the useful fiber plants of the world. Over one thousand species of plants contain useful fibers, but of this large number only about two dozen are heavily utilized.

Straw is seldom thought of as a fiber, but it finds use in the manufacture of hats and baskets and is often bunched up for packing fragile cargoes such as glassware. Most straw

consists of the leftover stems of the important grain plants
—wheat, oats, barley, rye and rice.

Various palms are valued throughout the tropics for
thatching shelters and making brooms, hats and baskets.
The best-known frond hat is woven from lead strands of the
panama hat palm. Even the stiff fibers found inside the husk
of a coconut find use as inexpensive stuffing and for mat
making.

An aspen grove in Colorado.

TIMBER PRODUCTS,
PAPER AND PLASTICS

TIMBER PRODUCTS

Next to foods that come directly from plants, timber is the most important plant product. Throughout most of the world wood is burned to provide warmth and is employed as a fuel for cooking. In many places charcoal, another wood product, is a primary cooking fuel.

Of course, the source of all heat in its various forms is the sun. This fact is most apparent while watching a log burning in a fireplace and feeling the radiating heat against the skin. This sensation is very similar to feeling the warmth of the sun's rays in summer. Burning is a simple way of releasing the sun's energy from wood.

Wood is also employed as a building material—for furniture, mining supports, boxes, railroad ties, barrels, fences, gates, tool handles, baseball bats and other sporting equipment, as well as violins, guitars and other musical instruments and hundreds of other products in our daily lives.

Plywood is presently popular for paneling and in the construction of such furniture as Ping-Pong tables, while veneers are used in fine furniture making and also for fine auto interiors. To produce thin, flat strips of veneer, logs stripped of their bark are rolled against a metal lathe that removes a thin layer of wood in a continuous strip. To produce plywood, "plies," or sheets, of veneer are glued on top of one another and bonded by a mechanical press.

While nearly all commercial plant products are derived from the large botanical class of flowering plants known as angiosperms, the world's timber supply is derived mainly from the conifers ("cone bearing") known as gymnosperms.

Soft coniferous woods are found chiefly in the northern regions of America, Asia and Europe. The Siberian forest contains one-third of the entire world's timber supply. The most important pulp-producing conifers of North America include white pine, Canadian spruce, pitch pine, red pine, jack pine and hemlock. Other softwoods of considerable use include Douglas fir, western red cedar and the two kinds of redwood.

WHITE PINE
CANADIAN SPRUCE
PITCH PINE
RED PINE
JACK PINE
HEMLOCK
DOUGLAS FIR
WESTERN RED CEDAR
REDWOOD

The redwoods are very scarce and nearing extinction in their native habitat of northern California. It is a sad statement that a civilization uses trees that may have been on earth since the time of Christ as slats for picnic tables and buckets.

OAK
MAPLE
BLACK WALNUT
BASSWOOD
ROCK ELM
ASH
COTTONWOOD
BIRCH

There are many more commercial hardwood timbers than softwoods, but they are generally scattered in smaller stands and available in much smaller quantities than softwoods. North American hardwoods include oak, maple, black walnut, basswood, rock elm, ash, cottonwood and birch. Uses include everything from boxes to baseball bats, violins to coffins. Even cork, which many think of as a product of the oceans, is derived from a hardwood tree.

Although most trees have a layer of cork beneath the outer bark, the cork oak is especially abundant in this lightweight material. These hundred-foot-tall evergreens are found growing throughout most coastal Mediterranean areas, but the largest commercial growing countries are Spain and Portugal.

CORK OAK

Good cork may be produced by some trees for as long as two hundred years. Usually the outer bark, or "corkwood," is peeled from the tree trunks every eight to fifteen years.

This process does not permanently damage the tree. As long as the inner bark is not cut, new layers of outer bark, or cork, will form over the years.

The ancient Greeks and Romans used cork for sealing bottles and for making the soles of shoes. Today cork goes into the manufacture of bottle stoppers, net floats, life preservers, artificial limbs, flooring, insulation and pin boards.

Some of the finest hardwoods come from the tropics and include African mahogany, African tola and greenheart. Teak is often considered the finest and most valuable of all woods. Its water-resistant quality is due to the large amounts of silica in its tissues. This dense and heavy wood is prized by ship builders, who use it mainly for decks, rails and cabins on many of the yachts manufactured today. Few commercial vessels have the large crew that would be necessary to maintain wood appointments. As a result, "modern" ships are made of metals and plastics.

AFRICAN MAHOGANY
AFRICAN TOLA
GREENHEART
TEAK

Honduras mahogany is a choice hardwood that has been used in making fine furniture ever since the famous eighteenth-century furniture maker, Thomas Chippendale, first created some of his masterpieces with it.

HONDURAS MAHOGANY

Balsa, another tropical hardwood, is even lighter than cork and is a favorite among model builders. It is also used in lifebelts, pontoons, sun helmets and hundreds of other products. Balsa is light because it contains very few wood cells and a great amount of air space.

BALSA

An unusual use for a tree product is the buttons and carvings that were formerly made from vegetable ivory. This ivory substitute was taken from seeds the size of chicken eggs found on the ivory palm, a shrub native to tropical America. Vegetable-ivory seeds are nearly pure cellulose and are therefore hard. This substance that once replaced true ivory or bone in umbrella handles, buttons, knobs and other products has itself been replaced by plastics. A limited amount is still used in native handicrafts such as carvings.

IVORY PALM

Okoume logs in Gabon being sorted for making plywood (top left). A huge lathe makes a long, continuous sheet of veneer by "unpeeling" log sections specially selected for plywood production (bottom left). A large paper mill in the United States (below).

PAPER

The Egyptians first used the woven stalks of papyrus reeds to make a writing surface about five thousand years ago. This early material, called *papyrus*, from which the word *paper* is derived, was rough and very difficult to produce.

About two thousand years ago a Chinese named Ts'ai Lun mixed the pounded fibers of hemp and mulberry bark together with cloth and water. After pounding them and squeezing out the liquid, he dried the thin surface in the sun. This produced a fairly good paper.

Eventually the Spanish learned to make paper, but instead of using the fibers of trees, they used cotton and linen rags as the chief ingredients. This was a very costly process. As the demand for cheaper paper increased, new sources were sought. Around 1850, Friedrich Keller, a German, learned how to use wood to make paper. This process was much less expensive than the linen-rag process and made it possible for millions of people to use paper as a writing surface. As a result of Keller's discovery, cheap paper became available and newspapers were printed on a mass scale.

Today the production of paper begins in the mill, where logs are rolled around together in a huge mechanical barrel until all the bark is dislodged. Then the logs are reduced to various sizes.

To produce the cheapest paper, known as "ground wood," logs are reduced to pulp on water-cooled grindstones. This pulp is then cooked or "digested" by chemicals in a huge vat to remove the substances that bind the cellulose fibers together. After washing and bleaching, the pulp is mixed at high speed in other vats until it has the consistency of porridge. Depending on the type of paper desired—writing paper, wrapping paper, newspaper or blotting paper—different materials are added to the stirred batch of pulp.

Next the liquid paper pulp is passed through large moving sieves that remove the water, leaving tiny fibers bound together in a sheet. These sheets are dried and pressed between huge steel rollers. To produce a glossy surface on paper such as that used in magazines and book jackets, a thin layer of clay and adhesive is applied in several coats in much the same way that paint is applied to a surface.

The watermark on fine paper is produced by inserting a design in the form of a wire mesh on the bottom of the paper mold that is passed between the huge steel rollers described above. This raised mesh creates less dense areas on the paper that may be seen when watermarked paper is held up to the light.

Today vast forests are cut down to produce the pulp necessary for making paper. About 40 per cent of all harvested timber is used for this purpose. The paper for just one Sunday edition of the *New York Times* requires the trees of twenty acres of forest.

To conserve trees, some manufacturers use recycled paper for books, newspapers, writing tablets, and such. This kind of paper is sometimes made from paper that has been used once or even twice before. It is made by chemically breaking down the old paper and then bleaching it to remove the print. The recycling of paper has been standard in the industry for many years. More than 20 per cent of the raw material of various paper products is derived from wastepaper. Some of the problems involved with using recycled paper are discussed in a publication of the American Forest Institute:

> One is that current waste pickup systems aren't geared to separate paper that can be used from paper that cannot. Ways must be found to dispose of old ink and coatings from the paper that is to be reused. And the recycling process can be more expensive than using new fiber. Finally, wood fibers lose strength each time they are reused. Therefore, recycled fiber must usually be bolstered by unused fiber.

If we hope to preserve our forestlands, we will have to use less paper. Paper cups and plates are wasteful, although convenient. Newspapers can be shared, as can magazines and books. Rags that can be reused many times can be substituted for paper towels, which are discarded after one wipe. The multitude of products that are now delivered packaged can be shipped loose, in bulk, and purchased unwrapped. In short, those who are serious about preserving the nation's forests must demand fewer forest products.

RAYON and PLASTICS

The commercial synthetic fiber known as rayon is produced from the cellulose fibers of wood pulp in a process that resembles paper making. The cellulose is not spread out in thin strips but is dissolved into a liquid by chemicals. It is then formed into very fine threads by passing through small holes in a metal spinner. This cellulose fiber is later hardened by removing the chemicals that first dissolved it.

Dissolved cellulose from cotton was formerly used in manufacturing one of the first commercial plastics, known as Celluloid. It was used to make cheap billiard balls and detachable collars for men. Today cellulose is removed from many different plants by use of various solvents. It is combined with other materials to make artificial leather and other valuable plastics that are used in the manufacture of thousands of products.

Before ending this section on the many uses of timber, it is essential to consider the usefulness of *living*, unharvested forests. Trees collect moisture and help to support the water table of adjacent farmlands. They act as excellent windbreaks and protect the soil. Trees are, after all, a pleasant sight in a not so pleasant world. Finally, forests support animal life that "tree farms" cannot maintain. Despite the claims made in advertising paid for by various lumber interests, when a forest is cut down, nearly all animal life in that forest disappears. No matter how "selectively" a forest is cut, the sound of heavy trucks and gasoline-powered saws drives away deer, birds, rabbits, beavers, chipmunks, squirrels, and other animals. Smaller animals are crushed beneath monstrous wheels. The soil is broken, erosion started, the balance of all forest life destroyed. A second-growth forest is just not the same as wilderness, in both emotional and biological terms.

Tapping a rubber tree in Ghana.

RUBBER, WAX, RESINS, GUMS AND DYES

Natural rubber from plant sources still plays an important role in the world's economy. Rubber motor mounts, washers, gaskets, rollers, hoses, belts, insulators and tubing are essential components of most machines. Soles and heels for shoes, waterproof garments, bottle stoppers, balls, bands, erasers and many elastic products are made of this substance. Rubber is essential to many of our activities and, of course, is used mainly in the manufacture of tires for automobiles, trucks, buses, airplanes and bicycles.

Few naturally derived waxes, resins, gums or dyes are economically important. Nevertheless, they are included because they are useful plants and may once again be called upon to supply man with the products described in this section.

Many of our waxes, resins, gums and dyes are presently manufactured from nonrenewable mineral and chemical resources that are becoming increasingly scarce. Plants, being living bodies, are "renewable" because their desired products can often be harvested without destroying the plants, and if the plant must be destroyed to gather the desired product, new plants can first be propagated from the previous generation.

RUBBER

When Europeans first explored the Amazon Valley, they noticed the Indians at play with elastic balls that bounced much higher than the "wind" balls then in use for playing games in Europe. The game-playing Indians could not foresee that later thousands of them would be enslaved and die at the hands of men desperate for the material out of which their bouncing toy was made.

Long before the arrival of Europeans, South American Indians had been using crude rubber to make shoes, water containers and other items. By 1600 shoes and clothing were being waterproofed by Spaniards and natives in tropical America.

When cured rubber was imported to Europe in the eighteenth century, it became a curiosity—used for little besides rubbing away pencil marks and for making toys. Its ability to remove the marks of lead on paper gave it the name *rubber*. It became known as India rubber because it was imported from the West Indies, islands in the Caribbean north of South America.

In the first half of the nineteenth century rubber came to be made into waterproof garments in Europe. Charles Macintosh, the inventor for whom some types of raincoats are still named, was first to utilize this strange material for its water-repellent qualities.

It was not until Charles Goodyear discovered how to prevent rubber from cracking in cold weather and softening in the heat of the sun that the demand for this material truly began. Goodyear found that by adding sulphur to it and heating, rubber undergoes a transformation that makes it impervious to the effects of a wide range of temperatures. He termed this process *vulcanization*, from Vulcan, the Roman god of fire. Eventually, vulcanized rubber became essential to the wheels upon which America's new invention, the automobile, began to roll.

Several kinds of plants exude a milky-white latex from which rubber can be made. Pará rubber from wild trees in tropical South America dominated the world's rubber industry until alternate sources were developed, first by cultivation of trees in the Far East and later by synthesis.

PARÁ RUBBER

It is believed that the Pará rubber tree produces much of its milky white juice as a mechanism to seal cuts in its bark. Removing this substance does not kill the trees, which can be tapped for up to twenty years. Other types of rubber trees—for example, Panama rubber trees—will die after being drained of their rubbery latex, and for this reason they never became important sources of natural rubber.

PANAMA RUBBER

To remove the milky juice for making rubber, cuts are made in the bark and the flowing latex is collected in little cups. Rubber workers then remove all the liquid from these cups and empty it into a larger container that is transported to the area where rubber is cured.

Before rubber can be used, it must first be separated from the remainder of the latex. In Brazil the latex is traditionally smoked on paddles over fires, which causes the rubber to form in layers. When somewhat dry, the caked rubber is cut from the paddles and hung up to dry until it is firm enough to be transported, usually in the form of large balls weighing as much as two hundred pounds.

Collected latex from cultivated rubber trees is cured differently. The milky substance is treated with acid until the rubber coagulates. It is then pressed through rollers until it is free of water. At this stage the sheet is smoked over fires of special woods to darken and preserve the rubber.

The great Far Eastern plantations of cultivated rubber trees were started with seeds of wild Pará rubber trees smuggled out of the Amazon in 1875. Until about 1912 Amazonian rubber still dominated world trade. Much wealth poured into Brazil, and entire cities flourished in the midst of the jungle. Manaus was one of the cities that boomed as the demand for rubber far outreached available supplies. The

In Brazil, a worker pours latex over a wooden paddle which is then
held over a smoke-box, until the latex turns into rubber.

city boasted an electric streetcar system, a palacelike opera house and many marble mansions. In 1907, at the height of the rubber boom, as many as five thousand men a week were coming upriver by steamer to Manaus to seek their fortunes.

By 1913 cultivated Malaysian rubber trees began to yield far more rubber per tree, and at a much lower cost, than the wild trees in the Amazon. Slowly men began to lose their fortunes in Brazil, and as the boom turned into a bust, the city of Manaus was slowly deserted. The city was eventually repopulated. Today some of the marble homes still stand, decaying and choked by the jungle's vegetation.

By far the greatest loss to Brazil was not men's fortunes. In the five years that Amazonian rubber was a monopoly product the population of forest Indians dropped from fifty thousand to eight thousand. Forced to work as slaves, the Indians were often left to die when they fell, creating "fields of bones." The entire story of the Amazon boom is told by Richard Collier in *The River That God Forgot*.

During World War II synthetic rubber was developed on a mass scale. When the Japanese invaded Malaysia and gained control of most of the world's rubber supply, the Allied forces had to find other sources to run a mechanized war. Chemists applied earlier knowledge and produced synthetic rubber from coal, petroleum and alcohol.

Since the cost of producing synthetic rubber is about equal to the cost of producing rubber from trees, equal amounts of synthetic and natural rubber are presently utilized throughout the world. Most tires are composed of a blend of natural and synthetic rubber. Most natural rubber still comes from Malayan plantations, while Brazil, the original homeland of the rubber tree, now accounts for a small fraction of the world's supply.

There have been other attempts to harvest rubber from plants and some of these latex-bearing species are listed in Table 6.

TABLE 6 Latex-Bearing Plants

PLANT	LOCALE	USES	PROBLEMS
Panama rubber tree	Central America to the Amazon	No longer utilized	Trees die when tapped
Guayule shrub	Texas and Mexico	Only during World War II emergency	Impurities in rubber
Mangabeira tree	Brazil to Paraguay	Rubber cement; waterproof cloth	Trees die
Landolphia vine	Equatorial Africa	Important only around 1900	Vines die
Russian dandelion	Russia	Could be used; no longer necessary	Plants die
Gutta-percha tree	India, Pacific Islands	Insulation for underwater cables; golfball centers	Not elastic; becomes brittle
Chicle tree	Mexico through northern South America	Made into chewing gum	Attempts to use it like rubber failed; later found application as chewing gum

WAX

Natural plant waxes today play a minor role compared to synthetic waxes or those derived from animals. They account for less than 3 per cent of all wax utilized throughout the world.

CARNAUBA PALM

Of all natural plant waxes, the one produced by the fan-shaped leaves of the carnauba palm of northern Brazil takes a higher polish and lasts longer than any of the others. Carnauba wax is one of the finest for automobile finishes and is also used in the manufacture of carbon paper, films, phonograph records, cosmetics, soaps, chalk, batteries, matches and crayons.

To harvest this wax, the leaves are cut and removed from the trees. As they dry in sheds, the wax falls off as a powder and is melted down and packaged.

Surprisingly, carnauba palms produce more wax during droughts than during periods of ample rainfall. It is thought that the palm manufactures wax to seal in its own moisture and thereby protect itself from the evaporating effects of heat. Because of the protection afforded by its wax, the carnauba palm is one of the few plants that survive in the semiarid conditions of coastal Brazil's northern savannah. Attempts to grow this palm on plantations have been economic failures, and all carnauba wax is harvested from wild trees.

Other wax plants include the bayberry, a source of candle wax; the candelilla shrub of northern Mexico; the cauassu herb of Latin American lowlands; the jojoba shrub of California and Arizona; and two or three other wax palms. None of these plants are under cultivation; all are found growing wild.

BAYBERRY
CAUASSU
CANDELILLA
JOJOBA

SOAP PLANTS

Many plants contain properties that enable them to be used as soaps. Their chemical makeup is due to the presence of saponins. In water saponins produce a froth, like soap, that traps fats and oils, thereby making saponin-containing plants useful cleansing agents.

Primitive peoples have long used natural soaps from the roots and barks of many plants. More than one hundred species in North America are known to have the qualities of soap without containing alkalies and metal salts. Vegetable soaps are presently popular among those who dislike caustic commercial soaps. Some natural soaps are made from the soapbark tree, soapberries, and occasionally from yucca roots, an old favorite of the desert Indians.

SOAPBARK
SOAPBERRIES
YUCCA ROOT

Natural soaps are distinguished from commercial soaps, which are produced by adding caustic soda and metal salts to plant oils such as coconut. Of all soaps made with oils coconut oil soap dissolves more quickly than the others. For this reason it is considered a highly soluble soap.

RESINS

While some plants generate rubber and wax to heal their bark injuries, most pine trees produce a sticky pitch on their cones, leaves and trunk that protects the tree through its antiseptic qualities. When boiled, this pitch breaks down into turpentine and rosin. Unfortunately, to get enough pitch from a pine tree to make the process economically worthwhile, the trunk must be "boxed," which seriously damages and eventually kills the tree.

Since ancient times the valuable properties of resins have been recognized. The Egyptians used resins to seal mummy cases, while other peoples found them useful for caulking the seams of boats. Resins also burn very well and were used to make all-weather torches.

Turpentine and rosin are the commercial products of pine resin. Rosin is used by bowlers and other athletes to "dry" their hands and by violinists to prevent their bows from slipping on the strings of their instrument. It works by increasing the friction between objects.

Resins are produced by many other plants, probably as a natural means for preventing decay. Amber, much sought after for jewelry, is a fossilized resin from extinct trees that formed after long burial in the ground. Botanists believe that amber is derived mainly from extinct pine trees. Most amber is dug out of the ground in Germany. In the vicinity of the Baltic Sea it sometimes washes up on beaches.

Amber is a fairly lightweight material that is worth its weight in gold. Prior to World War II a single piece weighing eighteen pounds was found that was later valued at $30 million. Amber is presently made into jewelry. Dr. Judith W. Frondel has described two simple means of distinguishing true amber from fake. When rubbed briskly, real amber gives off a pleasant odor, while fake material will often smell like camphor or singed rubber. Secondly, a real amber necklace will have beads of many different colors, while fakes usually are just one color.

GUMS

The gum arabic tree of North Africa, Arabia and India produces a gummy substance that is useful as a glue and in the manufacture of inks, polishes, and medicines. The outer "glaze" on candies is sometimes made of gum arabic. **GUM ARABIC**

This gum is occasionally tapped from small, twisted trees by nomadic African tribesmen. After the bark is slashed, the gum oozes out and is left to dry until collected.

Agar, a common solidifying agent for culture mediums on which microorganisms are grown, is produced by several species of red algae. After collection by divers, the seaweed is dried and then boiled to form a kind of jelly, the agar of commerce. This substance is also used in laxatives, as a thickener in foods such as ice cream and as a powder for fruit jellies. **RED ALGAE**

DYE PLANTS

Natural dye plants were once used extensively in the arts and for cosmetics. Synthetic dyes, developed mainly from coal tars, are now almost exclusively used for all coloring materials. The natural dyes are preferred by some people for historic or experimental purposes. There are some painters who use only natural pigments. In remote areas of the world most primitive people still use only natural dyes to color their masks, drums, weapons and bodies.

LITMUS LICHEN

Litmus paper, a chemical indicator of acids and bases, is made from the litmus lichen, which grows on cliffs from western Europe to South America. This natural dye is obtained by treating the tiny lichens with ammonia.

INDIGO
MADDER
ANNATTO

Among the hundreds of plant pigments are the beautiful blue indigo; the "Turkey red" madder, formerly used to color the pants of the French infantry; and the orange annatto, used as a food coloring.

LOGWOOD

One of the best-known natural dyes is made from the tropical logwood tree. This tree is native to Mexico but has been introduced throughout most tropical regions for its valuable dye. To gather the dark purple stain, known as haematoxylon, the trees are felled after ten to twelve years of growth. The heartwood is subjected to steam, boiled, or simply soaked in water. The dye is used for dyeing silk, fur, leather, wool and cotton products. Its greatest application, however, is in biology. Scientists use haematoxylon for staining cells that are to be viewed under the microscope. Thus far no synthetic substitute has been found that stains cells as well as this natural dye.

ARE PLANTS NECESSARY FOR OUR SURVIVAL?

We have now looked at some of the many useful products that are derived from plants. Beverages, foods, clothing, dyes, wax, rubber, paper, wood, tobacco, insecticides and many medicines, including birth-control pills, are but a few of these products. Looking around ourselves in every situation should reveal many other valuable derivatives of the vegetable kingdom.

It would be reassuring to leave our subject at this point, but before doing so, it may be useful to remember that the study of plants is "something more than a mere mental discipline," as Ronald Good has written. Although man's civilizations have evolved to a high level, the essential animal nature of his organism remains. He must still eat, maintain a shelter from the elements and rest. Further, "man's superior culture has *increased* rather than lowered his dependence [on the earth and the atmosphere] because it has so largely added to his wants. Diets are more varied, luxuries attain the status of necessities, clothing is essential, and far more is required to give the desired shelter and protection. . . . these things must be obtained by the exploitation of natural resources," including the plant world.

How secure may we be in assuming that these products will always be available to maintain our level of existence? Could we in fact continue to live if most plant life was in some way destroyed?

Let us look at the situation as we find it today.

Plastic lawns and aluminum Christmas trees do not spell the end of plant life on earth. They do announce the end of many traditions. In Europe plants once dominated works of art, coats of arms, coins and revenue stamps. Some American road signs situated in agricultural areas still carry messages to the Almighty requesting an abundant harvest. But the era of belief in faith as a method of relating to the management of all living things, plants included, is drawing to a close. We are entering into a period where "science" will absolutely dominate man's relationship to the world of living things, himself included. There is something of a continued interest in plants, animals and human values, but the dominant trend seems to be typified by an official of New York City who stated, "Who needs trees? I hate the woods. I love the feel of pavement beneath my feet."

A desire to escape from the tangle of nature has been characteristic of all civilizations. Forests are cleared, vegetation "controlled," towns and cities built. With the exception of a few nomadic tribes, most men view the forest or jungle as unknown and dangerous, while the clearing has been the symbol of security, orderliness, even godliness.

We have now reached the point of no return in our rush to create islands of security fenced against the great wilderness that once characterized this planet. The majority of men now congregate in these clearings. What remains of true wilderness is fast being requisitioned for lumber, agriculture or recreation. Paved highways are the roads to man's future—all leading to almost complete burial of much of the earth's natural terrestrial vegetation.

If we look at these "islands of security" that separate us from the wilderness, we can see that man's former orientation to the wilderness has undergone a complete reversal. The city is no longer considered orderly and safe, while the forests are looked upon as havens. Unfortunately, as masses of people rush "back to the wilderness," these havens become developed as suburban communities and eventually cities. As these areas become overcrowded and "used out," they too are abandoned.

As this process of urbanization continues and more of the earth's surface becomes buried, the survival of *Homo sapiens* will *not* be dramatically threatened. The quality of our food will continue to decrease, certain plant products such as paper will become scarce, and eventually tea, coffee, and tobacco, as well as many other natural products, will again become rare luxuries available only to those wealthy enough to afford them, but we will continue to survive.

Some have argued that we depend on plants for our oxygen and that we will slowly suffocate as the forests are denuded of their trees. This is not true. We do not depend upon terrestrial vegetation for our oxygen, nor do trees and lawns contribute any significant quantity of this essential gas to the atmosphere. Between 80 and 90 per cent of the oxygen we breathe is generated through photosynthesis conducted by plankton in the world's oceans. Some believe that oxygen may also be generated by reactions in the ionosphere.

What *is* being destroyed along with the disappearing plant life are many of the qualities of life that make it particularly human. A natural forest is somehow more inspiring, more restful, than a man-made park. An artificial lake stocked with selected fish and aquatic plants is somehow less exciting than a real lake filled with surprising creatures and turns and unexpected occurrences. An original forest is alive in ways that a replanted forest is not. A wilderness cannot be created and enjoyed in one lifetime.

If the destruction of wilderness areas continues, many of the subtleties of living will no longer exist and the death of earth's beauty may one day be sadly celebrated by our technicians and scientists, along with the rest of humanity who encouraged this destruction. Can poetry, music and the other arts survive a world no longer wild? Are those life processes and relationships that are well understood and described in textbooks to become the only survivors of the great world of life?

The forests, seashores and even the swamps are not only useful as they are but absolutely essential in ways we are slowly beginning to realize. Just as vitamins were once unknown necessities for true health, certain occurrences of the natural world that are as yet unknown may also be necessary for the maintenance of a healthy, enjoyable life, the true sign of civilized living. In the final analysis, then, plants are necessary for the survival of a *civilized* existence.

To maintain plants, our allies in the struggle of life, the supports and roots of our civilizations, we must purify the soil, air and water upon which they depend. The paving of miles of forest and grassland must be stopped; toxic levels of atmospheric contaminants must be reduced to facilitate the entry of sunlight and the exchange of gases; and the earth's oceans, lakes, rivers, streams and ponds must be cleansed. Only then can the essential useful plants of the world continue to grow in our service and for our pleasure while contributing to the maintenance of the semblances of civilization that remain.

ADDITIONAL READING

ANDERSON, EDGAR. *Plants, Man and Life*. Berkeley and Los Angeles: Univ. of California Press, 1969.

COLLIER, RICHARD. *The River That God Forgot*. London: Collins, 1968.

COOKE, DAVID C. *How Paper Is Made*. New York: Dodd, Mead & Co., 1959.

DODGE, BERTHA S. *Plants That Changed the World*. Boston: Little, Brown & Co., 1959.

EDLIN, H. L. *Man and Plants*. London: Aldus Books, 1967.

FRISCH, ROSE E. *Plants That Feed the World*. Princeton, N.J.: Van Nostrand Co., 1966.

FRONDEL, JUDITH W. "Amber Facts and Fancies," *Journal of Economic Botany* 22 (4):371.

GOOD, RONALD. *Plants and Human Economics*. London: Cambridge Univ. Press, 1933.

GRAY, ARTHUR. *The Little Tea Book*. New York: Baker & Taylor Co., 1903.

*HILL, ALBERT F. *Economic Botany*. New York: McGraw-Hill, 1952.

HVASS, ELSE. *Plants That Feed Us*. London: Blandford Press, 1966.

———. *Plants That Serve Us*. London: Blandford Press, 1966.

JACOB, HEINRICH E. *The Saga of Coffee*. London: Allen & Unwin, 1935.

JONES, L. W., ed. *A Treasury of Spices*. New York: American Spice Trade Assoc., 1956.

KREIG, MARGARET B. *Green Medicine.* Chicago: Rand McNally & Co., 1964.

MASEFIELD, G. B., *et al. The Oxford Book of Food Plants.* London: Oxford Univ. Press, 1969.

MEDSGER, OLIVER P. *Edible Wild Plants.* New York: Collier Books, 1972.

PAULING, LINUS. *Vitamin C and the Common Cold.* San Francisco: Freeman & Co., 1970.

SARGENT, FREDERICK L. *Plants and Their Uses.* New York: Henry Holt & Co., 1927.

*SCHERY, ROBERT W. *Plants for Man.* Englewood Cliffs, N.J.: Prentice-Hall, 1972.

ULRICH, ROLF. *Coffee and Caffeine.* Bristol, England: John Wright & Sons, 1958.

WEINER, MICHAEL A. *Earth Medicine—Earth Foods: Plant Remedies, Drugs, and Natural Foods of the North American Indians.* New York: Macmillan Co., 1972.

* Basic books that should answer most questions generated by reading this book.

INDEX

A

ABACA (*Musa textilis*), 110
Absinthe, 94
Accessory food plants, 10
ACEROLA (*Malpighia glabra*), 46
ACORNS (*Quercus* spp.), 27, 28
AFRICAN TOLA (*Pterygopodium oxyphyllum*), 115
Agar, 131
Alcoholic Beverages, 67, 77, 99·
ALFALFA (*Medicago sativa*), 23
ALGAE, RED (several spp.), 131
ALLSPICE (*Pimenta officinalis*), 65
ALMOND (*Prunus Amygdalus*), 28
Amber, 130
Angiosperms, 114
ANNATTO (*Bixa orellana*), 132
Antibiotics, 82–83
Arrow poisons, 81, 88–90
ARTICHOKE (*Cynara Scolymus*), 56
ASH (*Fraxinus* spp.), 114
ASPARAGUS (*Asparagus officinalis*), 56
AUTUMN CROCUS (*Colchicum autumnale*), 87
AVOCADO (*Persea americana*), 47

B

Bacteria, "nitrogen-fixing," 23
Bagasse, 40
BALSA (*Ochroma lagopus*), 115

BAMBOO (*Bambusa vulgaris*), 56
BANANA (*Musa* spp.), 47
BARBASCO (*Lonchocarpus nicou* var. *utilis*), 91
BARLEY (*Hordeum* spp.), 18–19, 77
BASSWOOD (*Tilia americana*), 114
BAYBERRY (*Myrica cerifera*), 129
Bean family, 22
Beans, 22, 24
Beer, 19, 67, 73, 77
BEET (*Beta vulgaris*), 56
BELLADONNA (*Atropa belladonna*), 87
Beriberi, 12
BETEL NUT (*Areca catechu*), 100
BETEL PEPPER (*Piper betle*), 100
Beverage plants, 67–78
BIRCH (*Betula* spp.), 114
Birth control pills, 84
Blood plasma substitute, 27
BRAZIL NUTS (*Bertholletia excelsa*), 27, 28
Bread, 10–11
BREADFRUIT (*Artocarpus altilis*), 48
BROCCOLI (*Brassica oleracea* var. *botrytis*), 56
BRUSSELS SPROUTS (*Brassica oleracea* var. *gemmifera*), 56
BUCKWHEAT (*Fagopyrum esculentum*), 20

C

CAAPI (*Banisteriopsis Caapi*), 87
CABBAGE (*Brassica oleracea*), 56
Caffeine, 67, 73, 74, 76
CALABAR BEANS (*Physostigma venenosum*), 90
CAMPHOR (*Cinnamomum Camphora*), 94
CANDELILLA (*Euphorbia antisyphilitica*), 129
Carats, 26
Carbohydrates, value of, 8
CAROB (*Ceratonia Siliqua*), 24, 26
CARROT (*Daucus carota*), 56
Cartier, 82
CASCARA (*Rhamnus* spp.), 87
CASHEW (*Anacardium occidentale*), 28
CASSAVA (*Manihot esculenta*), 36
CAUASSU (*Calathea lutea*), 129
CAULIFLOWER (*Brassica oleracea* var. *botrytis*), 56
CEDAR
    EASTERN RED (*Juniperus virginiana*), 94
    WESTERN RED (*Thuja plicata*), 114
CELERY (*Apium graveolens*), 56
Cellulose, 120
CENTURY PLANT (*Agave* spp.), 77
Cereals, 9–21
CHESTNUTS (*Castanea* spp.), 27, 28
CHICLE (*Achras zapota*), 128
Chippendale, 115
CHIVES (*Allium schoenoprasum*), 56
CHOCOLATE (*Theobroma cacao*), 58, 64, 67, 75, 76
CHRYSANTHEMUM (*Chrysanthemum* spp.), 92
CINCHONA (*Cinchona ledgeriana*), 86
CINNAMON (*Cinnamon zeylanicum*), 65

CLOVER (*Medicago* spp.), 23
CLOVER, SWEET (*Melilotus alba*), 23
COCA (*Erythroxylon coca*), 99
Coca leaves, 76, 99
Cocaine, 99
Cocoa, 67, 75, 76, 95
COCONUT (*Cocos nucifera*), 27, 28, 30
COFFEE (*Coffea arabica*), 58, 67, 73–75, 95
COLA (*Cola nitida*), 67, 76, 95
COLLARDS (*Brassica oleracea* var. *acephala*), 57
Columbus, 60
Cork, 114
CORK OAK (*Quercus suber*), 114
CORN (*Zea mays*), 18, 58
Cortez, 64
COTTON (*Gossypium* spp.), 103, 104–106
COTTON, SEA ISLAND (*Gossypium* spp.), 106
COTTONWOOD (*Populus* spp.), 114
CROCUS (*Crocus sativum*), 64–65
CURARE (*Chondrodendron toxicoferum*), 88

D

DANDELION, RUSSIAN (*Taraxacum kok-saghyz*), 128
DATE (*Phoenix dactylifera*), 51
DDT, 91
DOUGLAS FIR (*Pseudotsuga menziesii*), 114
DURIAN (*Durio zibethinus*), 51
Dye plants, 131–132
Dyes, 123

E

EGGPLANT (*Solanum Melongena*), 54
ELM, ROCK (*Ulmus thomasi*), 114
ENDIVE (*Cichorium Endivia*), 57
ERGOT (*Claviceps purpurea*), 87

Peruvian pottery, 26
PEYOTE (*Lophophora Williamsii*), 87
PINE
  JACK (*Pinus banksiana*), 114
  PITCH (*Pinus rigida*), 114
  RED (*Pinus resinosa*), 114
  WHITE (*Pinus strobus*), 114
Pine trees, 94
PINEAPPLE (*Ananas comosus*), 53
PISTACHIO (*Pistacia vera*), 29
Plastics, 113, 120–121
Plywood, 113, 116
Poison, 34, 36
Polenta, 18
POTATO
  SWEET (*Ipomoea batatas*), 35
  WHITE (*Solanum tuberosum*), 33–35, 58
Potato chips, 34
Primitive man, 1, 45, 81, 103
Protein-digesting enzyme, 53
Proteins, value of, 8
"Pseudo-cereals," 21
PULQUE (*Agave* spp.), 67, 77
PUMPKIN (*Cucurbita pepo*), 54
Pyrethrum, 91–92

Q
Queen Isabela, 60
QUINOA (*Chenopodium quinoa*), 21

R
RADISH (*Raphanas sativus*), 57
RAUWOLFIA (*Rauwolfia serpentina*), 87
REDWOOD (*Sequoia* spp.), 114
Reindeer, 7
Resins, 123, 130–131
RHUBARB (*Rheum Rhaponticum*), 57
RICE (*Oryza sativa*), 12–15

RICE, WILD (*Zizania aquatica*), 20
Root crops, staple, 33–37
Rosin, 130
Rotenone, 91
Rubber, 122–127
RYE (*Secale cereale*), 19

S
Saffron, 64–65
Shortages, plant product, 3–4
SISAL (*Agave sisalana*), 110
Soap plants, 129
SOAPBARK (*Quillaja saponaria*), 129
SOAPBERRIES (*Sapindus saponaria*), 129
Soft drinks, 67
Softwoods, 114
SORGHUM, SWEET (var. *saccharatum*), 43
SORGHUMS (*Sorghum vulgare*), 20, 43
SOYBEAN (*Glycine Max*), 24, 25
Spice Islands, 59–60
Spices, 58–66
SPINACH (*Spinacea oleracea*), 57
SPRUCE
  BLACK (*Picea mariana*), 82
  CANADIAN (*Picea glauca*), 114
SQUASH (*Cucurbita* spp.), 54
Staple food plants, 10
STROPHANTHUS (*Strophanthus kombe*), 90
SUGAR
  BEET (*Beta vulgaris* subsp. *cicla*), 41
  CANE (*Saccharum officinarum*), 39
  MAPLE (*Acer saccharum*), 42
  PALM (several genera), 43
Sugar refining, 40, 41
Survival, 133–137
Swiss lake dwellers, 107